D0955365

MUSIC'S GREAT DAYS
IN THE SPAS AND WATERING-PLACES

By the same author

JOHN DRYDEN
A Critical Biography

A. J. BALFOUR
The Happy Life of the Politician, Prime Minister,
Statesman and Philosopher, 1848–1930

CHURCHILL AND BEAVERBROOK
A Study in Friendship and Politics

RHODESIA AND INDEPENDENCE
A Study in British Colonial Policy

MUSIC'S
GREAT DAYS
IN THE SPAS AND
WATERING-
PLACES

Kenneth Young

MACMILLAN

© Kenneth Young 1968

Published by
MACMILLAN AND CO LTD
Little Essex Street London wc2
and also at Bombay Calcutta and Madras
Macmillan South Africa (Publishers) Pty Ltd Johannesburg
The Macmillan Company of Australia Pty Ltd Melbourne
The Macmillan Company of Canada Ltd Toronto
St Martin's Press Inc New York

Printed in Great Britain by
ROBERT MACLEHOSE AND CO LTD
The University Press, Glasgow

Library of Congress catalog card no. 69–12149

IN MEMORY OF

ALICE JANE YOUNG

my mother

who first introduced me to the
delights of music at the spa
'beside the idle summer sea
And in the vacant summer day!'

Contents

Chapters in which the chief resorts are referred to:
Bath 4; Bournemouth 12; Bridlington 8; Brighton 11; Buxton 10; Cheltenham 11; Eastbourne 9; Folkestone 10; Harrogate 3; Hastings and St Leonards 11; Llandudno 2; Margate 10; New Brighton 8; St Annes 8; Scarborough 5; Torquay 11; Tunbridge Wells 11; Weston-super-Mare 6; Weymouth 10; Whitby 11; Worthing 11

List of Plates

Acknowledgements

The publishers wish to thank the following for kind permission to reproduce the illustrations quoted by plate number:
Bridlington Public Library 25; Boosey & Hawkes 26; Camera Press 23; Cheltenham Public Libraries, Art Gallery and Museum 37; Daily Express 14; Eastbourne Public Libraries 35; Elgar Birthplace Trust 22; B. Hollins 7; G. E. Houghton Ltd 40; Illustrated London News 20; Geo Lord 29; Mander & Mitchenson 21; Mansell Collection/*Vanity Fair* 43; Maurice Miles 9; Photochrome Co. 24; Radio Times Hulton Picture Library 1, 3, 4, 8, 13, 17, 27, 41, 42; Royal College of Music 36; Scarborough Public Libraries 12; 'Snaps' 15; Tate Gallery 28; Torbay Library Service 30; Lambert Weston 31; Weston-super-Mare Borough Museum 18

Preface

In these pages, mainly historical, slightly nostalgic, I offer
something of the story of music – who played it, what they
played – at the spas and watering-places. Its hey-day was
between 1880 and 1950 when many resorts had large orchestras,
with first-class players, offering not only light music old and
new but classical symphonies and concerti and new compositions by English composers. Much of it is unexplored territory
with – except in the case of Bournemouth – few printed guide-
lines, so I have relied greatly on the generous communications
of elderly *aficionados*. Otherwise there are not many records;
programmes have seldom been preserved; council minutes
bleakly observe only that 'Mr X was appointed Musical
Director at £Y a week'. Yet once, not so long ago, thousands
flocked to the concerts of the Llandudno Pier Company's
Orchestra, the Duke of Devonshire's Eastbourne Orchestra,
the Spa Orchestras at Scarborough and at Buxton, the Hastings,
Whitby, Margate, Harrogate Municipal Orchestras. Some of
their conductors became celebrities – Basil Cameron, Sir
Malcolm Sargent, Sir Dan Godfrey, Sir Granville Bantock,
Alick Maclean, Maurice Miles. With them as soloists appeared
almost every great performer – and most English composers –
between 1880 and 1950. In later years the concerts became
familiar far and wide through their transmission by the
wireless.

All are vanished, depriving us (in my opinion) of a particular
kind of musical pleasure in surroundings themselves pleasurable. My aim here is to catch some of the echoes of the dead-

and-gone music of the spas and seaside places before they
finally fade into a harmonic empyrean beyond living memory.

Apart from all those public and private persons listed on
pp. 217–18 who have helped me, I warmly thank Miss Mary
Todd for her researches on my behalf and her meticulous work
on the manuscript, and Mr Simon Evers of Edinburgh
University.

KENNETH YOUNG

Chart Sutton, Kent

1. Prelude
The Harmonious Island

Music, the greatest good that mortals know,
And all of heaven we have below.

Joseph Addison, *A Song for St Cecilia's Day, at Oxford*

WITH much superior huffing and puffing, German musicologists in the late nineteenth century announced that England was a land without music. This dictum was meekly accepted. It was certainly true that England lacked the state-subsidised orchestras and opera houses of Germany, Italy and France; it may even be conceded that she could not boast a composers' roll-call as eminent as that of Continental Europe and Russia. But music itself burst forth in every corner of the land. There was much more 'live' music than today. It tinkled and warbled in homes, it thumped from brass bands in grim industrial towns. Across still summer evenings, catches and choruses sounded distantly from Glee Clubs in parish rooms. Cavernous town halls echoed with the swelling voices of great choirs. Almost every suburb had its 'Apollo Ensemble' varying from quartets to 'grand Victorian orchestras' of twenty-five to thirty performers, prominent among them being the local music teachers. Amid the greenery of the parks, the semi-tropical shrubs of the velvet-curtained Splendide Hotels, in every cafe and teashop,[1] music sounded. Musicians amateur and professional sawed and blew in assembly halls, church halls, skating rinks and at al fresco concerts in private grounds. There were *thés dansants* and musical soirées and, after about 1912, the picture palaces employed trios and larger combinations. In the great houses and the London drawing rooms, celebrated soloists, quartets and sometimes chamber orchestras were hired to play for guests after dinner.

Above all, the Briton craved music when he was on holiday or, as it was earlier called, taking the waters. From the late seventeenth century the spas had regular seasonal bands for the water drinkers, often as early as 7.30 a.m., for the balls and concerts in Assembly Rooms and elsewhere: in Bath such a band played every year from 1704 to 1939. When the seaside resorts began to flourish in the mid-nineteenth century, they had itinerant or small Town Bands, visiting regimental and brass bands. Later came the Blue Viennese, White Hungarian, Tzigane, Kossuth Hungarian, Meier's Viennese, essentially wind bands – their sound carried better across breezy Promenades – though there was usually a string element. Their leaders bore such names as Signor Enrico Scoma, Herr Kluckner, Herr Moritz Würm – preponderantly German,[2] although in later days there were many native players, the Scarlet Hungarian Band in Weymouth in the early 1920s being led by a Frank Harrington. They played operatic overtures and

---

[1] In 1923, Messrs Lyons spent £150,000 a year on teashop music, according to Sir Dan Godfrey (*Memories and Music*, London, 1924).

[2] Henry Mayhew in his *London Labour and the London Poor* (1861 edn., III 163) observed that the German bands had 'possession' of the whole coast of Kent and Sussex and wherever there were watering-places.

selections, waltzes and quadrilles, marches and galops, inter-
mezzos and ballet music, violin or trumpet solos and such
classics as 'Lucy Long' arranged for bassoon, or 'picture' music
of the simpler kind involving bells, spinning wheels, rustling
leaves or watermills. Their repertoire was mainly foreign;
not until the turn of the century did English light music
appear.

As the resorts grew, some of them attracted well-to-do
retired residents who wanted regular concerts with a wider
repertoire, including the classical symphonies. Usually this
meant having more players than the usual dozen or so of the
itinerant German band; for out-of-season concerts a hall was
needed in addition to the open-air concourse for summer. (In
France they ordered things differently: the Casino often
sheltered the Symphony Orchestra, the Cossack band, chamber
music and opera).

Eastbourne set the trend with its Devonshire Park Orchestra
in the mid-1870s, though there may be earlier examples since
records at all resorts are sparse and often non-existent.
Scarborough, Buxton, Harrogate, Llandudno and Bournemouth soon followed. Bath early tackled symphonies but never
with many more than twenty players, whereas the Eastbourne
Orchestra was up to fifty in the 1880s, followed by Bournemouth in the 1890s. Most resorts never rose to such heights.
Even so in the early twentieth century small, unlikely places
such as Whitley Bay, Saltburn, St Annes-on-Sea and Broadstairs boasted their seasonal pier, pavilion or municipal
orchestra. Some – though not always the smallest – never
attempted much beyond the lightest of music, and quickly
declined to shows and stunts rather than concerts. Other places
lacked continuity, pursuing a stop-go policy on the maintenance of such orchestras: for example Brighton. Most but not
all the resort orchestras were seasonal: winter for Bath,

Hastings and (latterly) Eastbourne; summer for all the northern resorts, except briefly Buxton, and for Margate, Weymouth, and the rest. Bournemouth had an orchestra all the year round, and so for a time did Folkestone and Worthing.

What caused this musical high tide at the watering-places? Social change had much to do with it. Railways had made travel easier and cheaper. Many more people could afford holidays away from home, and the bourgeoisie did not yet venture much into foreign parts. The seaside was fashionable even for the well-to-do. With the spread of education, interest in the arts generally was growing, but it was not always easy to satisfy, particularly in music. There was neither wireless nor gramophone. Outside London, Manchester and Glasgow there were no regular professional orchestral concerts. So that to hear a band of professional musicians was something new for most holidaymakers. It was part of the brief luxury of being on holiday; like being waited on, cooked for and idling in a deck-chair it was something that did not happen at home.

The newly-emancipated holidaying classes were not, however, ready yet for the solidly symphonic programmes of the Hallé or the triennial Leeds Festivals. They would have soon become bored. So the concert-promoters offered a mixed bag of items, mainly short and light. For the minority whose musical tastes were more developed, there was at some resorts a weekly symphony concert with a distinguished visiting soloist. This was the policy at Bournemouth, Harrogate, Eastbourne, Hastings and, at one time, Scarborough.

Some of the most successful of the orchestras, however, played a symphony in the middle of a programme that might also include a musical comedy selection, Bach's Suite No 3 in D, an Eric Coates descriptive piece ('Cinderella', 'The Three Bears'), the latest dance tune, and the overture to *The Flying Dutchman*. There was little educative intent. The aim was to

provide something for everybody – and no doubt to relieve the
boredom of the often highly skilled musicians. This was the
policy of Alick Maclean at Scarborough, Julian Clifford at
Harrogate, Jan Hurst at Blackpool, and Dan Godfrey at
Bournemouth. Today there are no orchestras offering such
mixed programmes. Yet as a *Times* leading article asked a few
years ago, 'Who wants masterpieces all the time?'

The resort orchestras were not the first – though they were
the last – to present such highly varied programmes. In the
early nineteenth century, Philippe Musard in Paris and the
elder Strauss in Vienna played concerts (in the open air in the
summer, in a hall in the winter) which, though rooted in dance
music, contained operatic selections, overtures and movements
from the symphonies. They appealed not to the select few who
supported the Conservatoire or Philharmonic concerts but to
the mass of town-dwellers bent on a light-hearted night out.
The arena was gay with flowering shrubs, fountains threw
'sparkling waters' among the glittering lights; there was space
to promenade and bars for the flagging spirits. The idea spread
to England where similar concerts were conducted by Pilati
at the Colosseum in Regent's Park, and by Negri at the English
Opera House (the Lyceum Theatre). At the Crown and Anchor
tavern Eliason gave promenade concerts with all the facilities,
introducing, too, whole symphonies as well as quadrilles and
waltzes.

It was, however, the arrival in England of the extraordinary
M. Louis Jullien between 1840 and 1859 that established what
may be called the resort tradition. Jullien himself, who ended
bankrupt and mad, I will not describe: this has been done to
perfection by Adam Carse[1] who tells us that Jullien was a
household word in all classes of society in Britain – as well-
known as Gladstone, Blondin, Captain Webb, Sanger's circus

[1] *The Life of Jullien* (Heffer, Cambridge, 1951).

or Wombwell's menagerie. More relevant here is the structure
of Jullien's programmes. At his public concerts – he played also
for dancing and *bals masqués* – he normally included classical
symphonies, Beethoven's in particular (though it is recorded
that he could not resist heightening the effects of the storm in
the 'Pastoral' by rattling dried peas in a tin box to simulate
hailstones). Jostled by ballads, polkas, quadrilles, operatic
selections and cornet solos (the *cornet-à-pistons* was newly
invented) would be a Haydn symphony, a Mendelssohn
concerto and even Berlioz's 'Harold in Italy'. Such programmes,
with a few composer changes, could have served as a model for
the resort orchestras, as they did for the promenade concerts
started by Henry J. Wood at the newly-built Queen's Hall in
1895. Only much later did the 'Proms' become concerts in-
distinguishable, save in price and rehearsal time, from any
other symphony concert.

The Jullien tradition was not confined to programme-
making. He initiated a conducting style. When he arrived in
London, an orchestral conductor was no box office draw. No
one went to *see* Sir Michael Costa, Sir Charles Hallé, or Sir
August Manns conduct – they went to *hear* the music they
conducted. It was the reverse with Jullien: audiences flocked
to watch him; what he played was of secondary importance.
Seaside audiences, too, preferred – though they did not always
get – some lively acrobatics from their conductors. They approved of Stanislaus Würm who led his White Viennese band
on Brighton Pier during the 1890s – incidentally, Gustav Holst
was his trombone player. Visitors, it is said, were roused to
ecstasy when he conducted Strauss waltzes, presumably as
much by Würm as by waltz.

Not all the mannerisms or methods of Jullien were adopted,
for example his habit of conducting from the middle of
his orchestra which was grouped around him. The resort

conductors preferred the Costa style with the conductor in front of (though, as we shall see, not always facing) the orchestra which was arranged in a semi-circle. Jullien had a gold chair into which he sank exhausted between items: a few imitated him. He wore white gloves to conduct – so did military band conductors until the 1930s. His flowing locks are still standard equipment for the contemporary maestro, oddly not for most of the resort conductors at least in the twentieth century.

Enough of conductors: what of the conducted? Some came from wind bands (not all military in the strict sense), others from the theatres or the touring opera companies. Later in the day some were tyro products of an academic musical education. Most of the resort players, however, were those who found themselves 'resting' and practically all musicians had compulsory 'resting' in the summer. It is a remarkable fact that in all Britain no symphony orchestras until 1930 engaged players on an annual basis, except the Bournemouth Municipal Orchestra and for shorter periods the Harrogate Orchestra under Julian Clifford. The Scottish Orchestra, for example, provided a full-time contract only for three months each winter. All other orchestras of symphonic status were brought together as required. The Royal Philharmonic Orchestra played at eight concerts a year, the Liverpool Philharmonic at twelve, the Hallé at about thirty-five; even Beecham's London Philharmonic Orchestra in its hey-day in the 1930s had no more than ninety or so engagements including the grand season at Covent Garden.

Until the B.B.C. founded its symphony orchestra on a permanent basis in 1930, it was the fortunate player who was able to divide his life between miscellaneous work in the cities in the winter and a steady job in a resort orchestra in the summer, or in, for example, Harrogate in the summer and

Hastings in the winter.[1] Too many players were chasing too few jobs. This is why the resort conductors could handpick their musicians from the best orchestral players in the land – and pay them accordingly.

[1] Much more of a real permanency was to be found in the cinemas. In 1929 the distinguished musical critic, Edwin Evans, wrote in *Music and Letters* that it had been estimated on the basis of union statistics that 'picture theatres are now providing between three-quarters and four-fifths of the paid musical employment in the country'. And by this same token 'it is further estimated that the cinema is the sole, or at any rate the chief, avenue by which music reaches three-quarters of the potential audience of the population'. I might add that the coming of the talkies did not kill cinema orchestras which in many cases became larger, and a stage feature.

2. Rivière and Dr Sargent: *Llandudno Pier*

I have a reasonable good ear in music: let us have the tongs and
the bones.

Shakespeare, *A Midsummer Night's Dream*

BETWEEN the resort orchestras and the Jullien tradition
there is another direct link, a human one, in the person of
Jules Prudence Rivière. As Rivière tells us in *My Musical Life
and Recollections* – now an extremely rare book – published in
1893[1] his was a colourful, not to say varied career. Born in
France in 1819 he had been violinist, bassoonist in the 12th
Regiment of Light Infantry – during which time a young
trombone player was court martialled and executed for striking
the bandmaster with his trombone – alto-ophicleidist and bass
drummer. He rose to bandmaster and later to conductor of
one of the Musard-type Winter Garden orchestras in the
Champs Elysées with eighty musicians.

He arrived in London knowing half a dozen words of English,
in 1857. At first he copied music for Jullien and later conducted

[1] Sampson Low, London.

the band and 'spectacle' at the Cremorne Gardens.[1] This, he tells us in his autobiography, was a most arduous existence; he conducted an open air concert from 5 to 6 o'clock and from 7 to 8 o'clock there was a ballet for which he had to write the music; from 8 to 11 in the evening there was dancing followed by fireworks after which the dancing went on until 2 a.m. or even later – in June and July, indeed, until dawn.

Rivière became a music publisher in partnership with Hawkes, later of Boosey and Hawkes. He played in the theatres, buying up the rights of Offenbach's *La Belle Hélène*. At the Alhambra he performed great operatic selections, 'a few pretty pieces and the two regulation ballets'; he got together a reed band for the Light Cavalry of the Honourable Artillery; in 1871 with an orchestra of eighty he began 'Rivière's promenade concerts', frequently deploying a chorus of forty voices and a forty-strong military band made up from the Royal Artillery and the Grenadier Guards – one of whose bandmasters was Dan Godfrey, Senior.

He composed polkas and was one of four collaborators who wrote music for an operetta called *Babil and Bijou*. Rivière's song 'Spring, Spring, gentle Spring' was a hit, whistled in the street, rattled out by every organ-grinder.

Vividly he recalled one of his conducting colleagues, de Billemont, who was

> short and stout, and being also lame, [he] used a heavy walking stick, for support as we all thought and this he invariably kept close to him at the desk during practice. It soon became apparent that de Billemont walked out of the orchestra at the end of the rehearsals with the unsteady gait of a drunkard, albeit he came in every day perfectly sober, and never left his post during the performance. Mystified by the matter, the management set a watch upon his movements and he was seen several times during the rehearsal to gently

[1] See Chapter 3 below.

unscrew the head of his formidable walking stick, put a small tube into it, and then introduce the tube into his mouth. The walking stick contained rum.

After a successful Covent Garden season in 1874, Rivière took his orchestra on tour to Manchester, Edinburgh, Glasgow, Newcastle, Brighton, Birmingham, Nottingham, Southampton, Bath, Hastings and Liverpool. In 1877 he gave four grand orchestral concerts at the Westminster Aquarium. His promenade concerts at the Queen's Theatre in that same year were, however, a failure and his orchestra was not paid – in fact the directors and manager skipped, according to Rivière's account, with all the money. Rivière – already 62 – now retired to Lancashire and became conductor in 1881 at the Winter Gardens in Blackpool. It was, however, not there but at the North Wales resort of Llandudno that he became famous and qualifies for entry into these pages. Llandudno, lying cosily between the limestone headlands of Great Orme and Little Orme on a peninsula formed by the Irish Sea and the Conway river, had been no more than a fishing village until about 1860, but it had grown rapidly into a health and holiday town with golf courses, Alpine displays, a magnificent marine drive and steamers regularly bringing holiday makers from Liverpool.

In Llandudno in 1887 Rivière had an orchestra of thirty-six musicians. They could not be fitted into the open-air octagon bandstand at the pier head. So Rivière proposed to take them into the Pavilion itself which was very large. But the directors of the Pier thought that visitors would not – even for 'good music' – consent to be shut indoors on fine summer evenings. However, Rivière had his way: every evening a concert was given in the pavilion and the orchestra flourished, becoming well-known far beyond North Wales.

Rivière became a leading citizen of the town and was honoured by a banquet in 1889 at which Lord Mostyn took

the chair and presented him with an inscribed silver punch
bowl and ladle which became, he said, 'one of my most precious
possessions'. He settled down and built a villa for which one
of his Welsh friends gave him a name 'Bodalaw', the abode of
melody. The storm and stress of his life seemed to him to be
over. He was wrong. Although the concerts continued to make
money and 12½ per cent was paid to the shareholders in 1891
and in 1892, nevertheless there were differences of opinion –
unspecified – between him and the directors of the Pier. The
result was that at the age of seventy-four or so he departed
from the Pier and set up in a hall built for him and called
Rivière's Concert Hall. He continued to work there for several
more years, finally departing to conduct an orchestra at
Colwyn Bay. There one day after Christmas in 1900 he
died.

It is in his days at 'Rivière's Concert Hall' that we catch a
glimpse of him through the eyes of the young Henry J. Wood –
an unflattering glimpse (Wood was seldom kind, even to
elderly rivals). Wood's father had recommended the ambitious
young man, soon to take over the languishing 'Proms' in
London, to go to Llandudno to listen to Rivière. Wood's first
impressions gave him 'the shock of my life'. He says in his
autobiography, *My Life of Music*:

> As I took my seat I saw an elderly gentleman seated in a
> gilded armchair, *facing* the audience. He was elegantly
> dressed in a velvet jacket on the lapel of which reposed a
> huge spray of orchids more fitted for a woman's corsage.[1]
> He held a bejewelled ivory baton in his hand from which
> dangled a massive blue tassel. This he wound round his
> wrist. He bowed ceremoniously to the audience and tapped
> loudly on his golden music stand. Still seated, he began the

[1] Sir Dan Godfrey tells us that Rivière received so many floral offerings
from his fair admirers that he had a special collar made for his coat to hold at
least twenty buttonholes.

Overture to *Mignon*. After two bars a hoarse voice from the side of the orchestra said: '*Six* beats in a bar, please!'

This was unfair. By this time Rivière was an old man, but certainly he had conducted Ambroise Thomas's overture to *Mignon* thousands of times and knew perfectly well how many beats to give in the opening bars. As for the rest of the 'shock' it derived from the Jullien tradition: though Jullien never sat down to conduct, one of his successors, Luigi Arditi, did on a high stool but facing the orchestra.[1] Wood might also have mentioned that before Rivière began to conduct a uniformed and beribboned commissionaire handed him his baton and white gloves on a silver salver.

Young Wood's visit to Llandudno was not quite wasted. Having fled from Rivière, he went to the Pier where an orchestra under Bartlett[2] was playing to a packed house. The leader of the orchestra was Arthur W. Payne who played two movements from Mendelssohn's Violin Concerto and attracted Wood by the beauty of his tone. He then and there, he says in his book, made a note that if ever he wanted a leader he would offer the post to Payne, and so before long he did.

This was by no means the end of Payne's connection with Llandudno. Bartlett (or Bartle) departed to be followed for a brief period by Gwilym Crowe, composer of the 'See-Saw' waltz then all the rage. A year or two later Payne was appointed conductor and remained for some twenty-five years with an orchestra of considerable size – it varied between about thirty-four and forty-four, being biggest at the height of the season in

---

[1] To face or not to face the orchestra: Jullien, of course, did both since he stood in the middle of his orchestra which itself was in the middle of the hall. Conducting with back to the orchestra must have presented difficulties, though it was not uncommon in these early days. The tradition has lingered: the conductors of the large dance bands of the 1930s often beat time smiling at the audience. For National Anthems some conductors still turn to face the audience.

[2] I think Wood may have got the name wrong; it was probably A. E. Bartle.

August. He gained an enormous following in the town. Like
Arditi he directed the orchestra from a sitting position on an
extremely high chair facing his orchestra. At the end of each
work he somewhat disdainfully inserted the next number in a
slot behind the chair.

Payne is said to have been a typical Edwardian, a gentleman,
and a Fellow of the Royal Academy of Music. His band was
largely composed of members of the Hallé Orchestra including
(in later years) such well-known names as Alfred Barker, John
Bridge, H. Fawcett, W. Warburton the cellist, the two
Whittaker brothers on oboe and cor anglais, F. Gomez as
clarinet and one of the Draper family, P. B. Draper, as chief
bassoon player. His programmes were mixed after the Jullien–
Rivière recipe, though at weekends or on special occasions he
produced near-symphony concerts with celebrated soloists in
violin concertos, those of Bruch and Mendelssohn being
favourites. Moiseiwitsch, Beatrice Harrison, Wilhelm Backhaus, Marie Hall, Bratza and Jelly D'Aranyi all performed for
him at the Pier Pavilion.

The morning performances, if the weather was fine, took
place in the open air, the band being seated in a rotunda-type
building at the pier head. During the intervals the musicians
rushed off either into the sunshine or into the bars. They were
summoned back to duty by a fortissimo attack on the bass
drum by H. A. Dunn, who was also the orchestral librarian.

Towards the end of 1925 the Pier Company decided that a
change was needed to put new life into the concerts and to
attract more support. When, however, it was known that
Arthur Payne was to be dispensed with, there were protest
meetings in the town and no less than £1,200 was collected
by the patrons as a testimonial to him.

He was succeeded in 1926 by a slim young newcomer to the
resort orchestras, none other than Dr Malcolm Sargent. Some

of the old hands in the orchestra and the regular patrons, many of whom had attended Payne's concerts for almost as long as he himself had conducted them, were at first cold and hostile to the newcomer. Sargent was quite aware of the fact but he was determined to improve the orchestra by getting rid of some of the more ancient stalwarts and appointing young players, increasing the total from thirty-four to forty-four. This resulted in torch-light processions of protest up and down the Great Orme. Indignation mounted almost to frenzy when Sargent scrapped the sacred morning programmes and played Beethoven symphonies.

Before long, however, Sargent won over both the players and the public; it was recognised that the quality of the music played as well as the playing itself had improved. With the orchestra he was strict but human and had a sense of humour; he also had a complete mastery in handling his forces. Even the fact that he insisted on rehearsals was eventually accepted.[1]

Unhappily only a few of Sargent's programmes, which now have a biographical as well as historical interest, have survived. But one or two are before me. One September day in 1926, his morning concert included movements from Beethoven's Seventh Symphony, a Fantasia on the music from Wagner's *Master Singers* and two small pieces by Cowen, along with the usual marches, overtures and ballet music. In the evening more elaborate works were often played. On Sunday, 5 September 1926 – admittedly it had been described as a special concert – Sargent gave Elgar's 'Enigma' Variations and Constance Willis sang a song by Granville Bantock. One of Sargent's own works, Nocturne and Scherzo, was performed. On the following Thursday evening he conducted the Woodland Murmurs from Wagner's *Siegfried*, Siegfried's Funeral March and Schubert's

---

[1] One curiosity of his orchestra was that the harpist, H. Jarvis, was also a horn player – a doubling seldom if ever met with elsewhere.

'Unfinished' Symphony as well, again, as one of his own works, *Valsette*, for full orchestra, composed while he was an organist, and part of a seven-movement setting of Shelley's 'Ode to a Skylark'. This was one of the works that had helped to get him his Doctorate of Music at Durham University when he was 24 – the youngest Doctor of Music there had ever been in Britain.

One of the first to start – and with what *réclame*! – the Llandudno Pier Company's Orchestra was also one of the first to end at least as a full-scale orchestra, though a smaller combination, under the violinist John Morava, has continued to play for the last thirty years. Sargent departed after two seasons; for him a resort orchestra was no more than a stepping-stone. John Bridge, his leader and deputy, took over until he in turn went to the B.B.C. as the director of the nonet that took the place of the North Regional Station Orchestra during the economic 'freeze' in 1930.

The Pier Company cast about for a successor and found him in George Cathie, then 52, who had been leader and deputy to Norfolk Megone with the Devonshire Park Orchestra in Eastbourne from 1914, and conductor of the Buxton Pavilion Gardens Orchestra and of the North Pier, Blackpool, Orchestra. Cathie came of a Scottish-North Country family not unconnected with the arts – his mother was a painter and cousin of Francis Thompson the poet; his brother Philip – sponsored in his 'teens by a Bradford businessman – became Professor of Violin at the Royal Academy of Music in London. Both played in the Queen's Hall Orchestra and at Covent Garden, George forming his own chamber music quartet.

Of George Cathie's genuine love of music there is no doubt, nor of his willingness to encourage young English composers such as Patrick Hadley (later Professor of Music at Cambridge University) whose symphonic poem, 'Kinder Scout', he rehearsed and performed at Buxton. Dr Adrian Boult, then B.B.C. Director of Music, admired his work and put his Llandudno Orchestra frequently on the air to play the classical symphonies – and such rarities as the Norwegian Ole Olsen's Suite for Piano and Strings.

Cathie looked the part – and was, therefore, 'suspect'. Off the platform, he wore a black sombrero and a scarlet-lined black cloak. His baton was long, his gestures dramatic though quite unselfconscious. His hair was thick, leonine and in latter days white, his dress immaculate. His style has been compared – by his daughter – to that of the American–Jewish conductor, Leonard Bernstein. He had a fondness for long extracts from *The Ring* though, like some other of the good resort conductors, he could enjoy himself in the latest dance measure, an Alpine Fantasy (arr. Thurban) or a Waldteufel waltz.

For all that, he was a true musician, with a real interpretative gift. Present at one of his Buxton concerts in the early 1920s was the veteran composer, conductor and teacher, Sir Charles Villiers Stanford. Cathie had been performing a Brahms symphony and Stanford went backstage afterwards to congratulate him. Stanford, who had known Brahms personally, referred to a certain passage in the symphony:

'I noticed that you took it *ritardando*, which is not marked in the score: why was this?'

Cathie answered that he was particularly fond of Brahms's music which he had studied deeply, and he felt that this passage required a slight '*rit*' although it was not indicated in the score.

Stanford then told him that he had gone through the score of the symphony with Brahms, who had himself made that same '*rit*' when conducting it. Stanford had asked Brahms why he did not, therefore, mark it in the score, and Brahms replied:

'If I write it in, some of these fellows I know will make a great *allargando* of it! No, I prefer to leave it to the conductor's sense of the music.'

Stanford asked for Cathie's score and pencilled in the '*rit*', 'as interpreted by J. Brahms', and signed his name to it, saying 'Now you will have something to show if anyone ever criticises you as a young conductor taking liberties with Brahms!'

However fine the foregoing may have been, the last act is always bloody, as Pascal observed about life and as I shall be obliged to observe constantly about the resort orchestras. What happened to Cathie at Llandudno is typical of nearly all the rest.

In his 1935 season at Llandudno a deputation from the Directors of the North Pier, Blackpool – where he had spent four years – came to see Cathie. They offered him an improved concert pavilion, a larger orchestra and an increased salary if he would return. Meanwhile, the Directors of the Llandudno Pier Pavilion, despite the fact that takings had gone up by leaps and bounds under Cathie, were casting envious eyes at the packed audiences, though in a much smaller hall, at the rival Variety Show along the front. This being so, Cathie saw the Llandudno Directors and put his offer from Blackpool before them. He told them he was happy at Llandudno and confident that the Pier Pavilion Orchestra would continue to build up its audiences and prove that good music could still pay. But as he knew there was some feeling among Directors that the Pavilion ought to change to variety, he would be grateful if they could let him know whether this was likely in the near future, so that he could decide on the Blackpool offer.

He was assured that the Directors had no plans for a change, that they were more than satisfied with his work, and hoped he would remain at Llandudno. Cathie refused the Blackpool offer.

Early in the next year, much too late for other summer arrangements to be made, he heard from the Llandudno Directors that they had reluctantly decided there was no future for the orchestra at the Pavilion and were changing over to variety and dancing in the coming season. There was no redress – the contract had been seasonal, and there was nothing in writing from the 'reassurance' meeting. The war was to put an end to it all in another four or five years anyway, but there could have been a good four or five seasons had he gone back to Blackpool.

Such, I fear is the regular pattern, though this is a particularly gross example. Cathie never conducted a resort orchestra again. During the war he became musical supervisor for Poplar and Bromley Town Council's park entertainments. Afterwards he retired to Ewell in Surrey with his violin and his books, his water-colour paints and his roses.

3. Heavenly Harrogate:
Adams to Cameron

Was it a vision, or a waking dream?
Fled is that music . . .
                    Keats, *Ode to the Nightingale*

FROM water came Harrogate – water, imbibed or bathed in, and either way said by a writer in the early nineteenth century to have a salutary effect on diseases of the skin, to cure ulcers, old strains, aches and paralytic debilities and to destroy worms. Water plus Harrogate, he claimed, was 'an antidote to the blue devils, ennui and low spirits'. Against, in fact, melancholia.

From early days, however, it was generally recognised that the waters required to be supported, fortified one might say, by other therapeutic devices. Music for example because, as Robert Burton declared in *The Anatomy of Melancholy* in 1621: 'Music is a roaring-meg against melancholy, to rear and revive the languishing soul; affecting not only the ears, but the very arteries, the vital and animal spirits, it erects the mind and makes it nimble. This it will effect in the most dull, severe and sorrowful souls, expel grief with mirth.' Burton (quoting Cassiodorus) was certain that 'divine music' not only expelled grief but extenuated fears and furies and abated heaviness. It took away spleen and hatred 'be it instrumental, vocal, with strings, wind'. In addition it ravished the soul, the queen of the senses 'by sweet pleasure (which is an happy cure)'.

Possibly Harrogate needed psychosomatic music more than some other spas such as those in the West Country which had milder climates. Harrogate is on the edge of a blusterous moor. Sydney Smith, the Whig parson and wit, who once held the living of Foston in Yorkshire, referred to the place at the beginning of the nineteenth century as 'just three gaunt trees – and each of them bending *away*'. A little earlier the dyspeptic novelist Smollett (who might have benefited from a *régime*) described it as 'a wild common, bare and bleak, without any signs of cultivation'. One must confess to some wonder that this bleak, cold town should have been chosen by generations of valetudinarians and as a place of retirement by those of advanced years. It is not as if the waters were pleasant; they were nasty enough to please a masochist. The first of eighty-eight different springs, discovered as long ago as 1571 by a member of a still-celebrated Yorkshire family, William Slingsby, who knew the waters of Spa near Liège in Belgium, tasted foul. It was composed, we are told, of calcareous earth with projected crystals of a calcareous glauber-salt, and while mixing freely with milk, curdled soap. Sulphur wells, discovered later, stank: 'The popular opinion is, that Harrowgate water tastes like rotten eggs and gunpowder; and though it is probable no person ever made trial of such a mixture, the idea it conveys is not inapplicable.' But Dr Timothy Bright, writing in about 1597, referred to Slingsby's well as 'the English Spa' and in so doing added a new noun to the language. (In

Yorkshire 'spa' was until recent times pronounced, and sometimes spelt, 'spaw'.)

In the early part of the nineteenth century some 2,000
individuals visited Harrogate during the season and they were
'like one happy family, and misanthropy is put in good humour
in spite of itself', writes a chronicler of the time. Mainly they
came from

> the landed families of the north, country squires from the old
> stone granges of the Yorkshire Dales, and the moors and
> fells farther north, who came to tone up their constitutions
> with a few weeks in the bracing air of Harrogate, and, if
> their joints were beginning to creak, to undergo a course at
> the baths before returning to manage their estates – to sit
> on their benches, bully their parsons, ride to hounds and
> drink their pints with their tenant farmers, of an evening.

Board and food were also cheap which is perhaps why
Harrogate was much favoured from the early days by Scots
who used it as a half-way stop between Edinburgh and
London. Breakfast could be had at a mere tuppence a piece for
muffins (it was the custom for the ladies to bring their own tea
and sugar). Dinner was a shilling; supper sixpence; and
chambers free. Afternoon tea was given by each lady in turn;
this might have been thought an imposition but the turn came
round usually only once in four or five weeks.

Even so, 7.30 in the morning, the regular time for visitors
to troop to the springs, was a cold and dismal hour. Music
was the answer! So, soon after the Pump Room – now a
museum – was built and the Montpelier Baths opened, the
High Harrogate Band, composed of a harp, violin, clarinet,
flageolet and 'cello, played before breakfast near the Granby
Hotel and the Slingsby well. By 1845 a band was playing every
evening in the season on the Green. Who and quite what these
bands were is not clear; probably they were largely itinerant,

coming and going at street corners and outside shops; some were foreigners, some local players. While London was entertained by the music of Handel and Mozart and Haydn, the provinces were still dependent, apart from church music and the occasional festival, on the self-taught musician in the unorthodox combination.

Of such at the end of the eighteenth century Harrogate possessed an outstanding example in Jack Metcalf, better known as Blind Jack of Knaresborough. He was, it seems, a considerable fiddler as well as soldier, road-maker, bridge-builder, carrier, guide, huntsman; he could also play the hautboy (oboe). He was present as an Army bandsman at the Battle of Falkirk in 1745 when the Young Pretender was in full march towards Derby and the crown of England.

Blind Jack played for the quality in Harrogate, frequently at the Royal Oak Hotel in High Harrogate – later known as the Granby – where the story goes, the landlord's daughter fell for his musical charms. Jack discovered this but, owing to the disparity of her circumstances and his own, could not believe he had the right to follow any advantage this might offer. His apparent indifference so offended the young lady that in a pique she accepted the advances of a well-to-do admirer. On the day before the wedding Blind Jack addressed her:

'Well lass, thou's going to have a merry day tomorrow, and I'm going to be the fiddler.'

'Thou never shall fiddle at my wedding,' replied she.

'What's the matter, what have I done?' said the startled man.

'Matters may not end,' was her rejoinder, 'as some folks think they should.'

'What!' he exclaimed taking his cue, 'Hast thou rather have me – canst thou bear starving?'

'Yes,' she said, 'with thee, lad, I can!'

'Give me thy hand then, lass! Skin for skin, it's all done!'

So Blind Jack ran away with pretty Miss Benson, the publican's daughter. Asked later why she had refused so many good offers for the sake of Metcalf, she replied, 'Because I could not be happy without him.' The power of Harrogate music is abundantly demonstrated.

By 1835 at the Cheltenham Rooms in Harrogate, built by John Williams, there were nightly concerts and occasional morning recitals of high quality. Performers such as Thalberg, Sontag, and Lablache came from London – Thalberg whom Liszt acclaimed as 'the Prince of pianists', Henriette Sontag for whom Beethoven had written soprano parts in his operas, Lablache for whom Schubert wrote songs.

The vogue for band music reached the town and in 1868 the local paper observed: 'We are glad to record that the musical element of the entertainments of this watering-place is kept up to a proper standard. The programmes selected by Mr Julian Adams the conductor and solo pianist are really first class, and the manner in which they are rendered both by the orchestral and military bands is unexceptionable. The company of Harrogate seem also to highly appreciate the music presented to them.' Julian Adams, incidentally, is one of the few spa musicians to be included in *Grove's Dictionary of Music and Musicians* (at least in the current edition). He was a Londoner born in 1824, a composer and the man who introduced into England Debain's harmonium for which he published a Method in 1855. In 1851 he assembled an orchestra which gave a series of weekly concerts at Edinburgh, Glasgow and Greenock. He played in Paris and formed a touring orchestra in 1855 visiting Scarborough, Tynemouth and Buxton before settling in 1877 as conductor of the Devonshire Park concerts at Eastbourne where ten years later he died.

Harrogate loved him, the papers referring to him as 'our deservedly popular director. All admirers of the divine art who regularly attend the room know full well that these concerts are, upon the whole, the most uniformly unexceptionable to be found in England. Each programme contains a variety of the most popular and national as well as classical music. By this arrangement Mr Julian Adams suits his programmes to the most fastidious tastes; indeed, here is the secret of his power as a conductor.' Adams is also reputed to have been a wit, though the only extant example is not convincing. One day he was playing a melody on the piano in unison or at the octave with Mr Walton, a 'cellist who appeared unable to hit the right tempo. He was always ahead of the conductor-pianist. At length this so irritated Adams that he said: 'If you do that again, Mr Walton, you'll be Mr Walker.'

Other names appear from the mists. In 1875 there were 'Spa Promenade Concerts' conducted by Mr H. Cohen; in the 1880s there was a Harrogate Promenade Orchestra which seems to have been made up of sixteen players, most of them called Dearlove. The Dearloves are not so misty: they were a family of instrumentalists and instrument makers from Leeds and known from the eighteenth century. Mark Dearlove, violin maker and violinist, was born about 1790 and his son Mark William Dearlove, in the same trade, had eight boys – the girls are not recorded – all of whom were players, flautists, contra-bassists, cornettists and violinists. These in turn had children who played, as well as the above instruments, harps and drums. Their names are to be found in many of the orchestras of the nineteenth and early twentieth century and not merely in their native West Riding.

In Harrogate, music became more and more popular – and the musicians more hard-worked. Not all of it was 'good' music, at least not in the eyes of a condescending London paper, the *Pall Mall Gazette* in 1884: 'The entertainments are fairly well looked after, the Spa concert rooms and Gardens taking the lead. The orchestra in connection with this establishment, which has helped to pass away the morning hours, while the subscribers sit and talk, and read, and knit, performs in the concert room in the evening, and generally executes a "popular" programme very creditably. Of course, the instrumental portion of the concert must be relieved by a vocalist and for this purpose a third-rate *prima donna* has to be imported from London. If the lady be wise her programme will deal principally with kisses and kissing, and she will be enthusiastically encored. Fireworks are liberally introduced and are timed to waken children and invalids at 9.15 or thereabouts.'

Great things, however, were in the making for Harrogate, the Golden Age of its music about to begin. It was heralded by an insignificant, irrelevant but perhaps symbolic report in the local paper that at a grand concert to commemorate Queen Victoria's Jubilee of 1887, 'Mr Delius of Harrogate charmed the audience with his violin solos'. (The future composer, then twenty-five, lived with his wool-merchant parents in Harrogate.)

More immediately important were a series of articles by W. H. Breare, editor of the Harrogate Herald claiming that if Harrogate had its own band, rather than depending on 'any body of itinerant musicians' it would draw visitors to the town and lure them into extending their stay. Impressed, prominent citizens subscribed £400, and a Mrs Kaye-Knowles offered to equip a band at her own expense with a uniform to be designed and manufactured by W. G. Allen, a tailor of Prospect Crescent in Harrogate. A bandmaster was chosen in the person of J. Sidney Jones, at that time both conductor of the orchestra at the Grand Theatre in Leeds and bandmaster of the Leeds Rifles; with him in Harrogate was his son Sidney, the player of the E flat clarinet, who subsequently achieved fame as the composer of operettas such as *San Toy*, *The Geisha*, *A Greek Slave*, *See See*, and *The Girl from Utah*.

J. Sidney Jones, *père*, with his steady beat and luxuriant moustache, has two claims to fame. Against odds he turned what was essentially a military band into an orchestra capable of playing the classical symphonies, and he compelled a hesitant municipality to undertake financial responsibility, though at first they thought that they should pay half the salaries, leaving the rest to collections from audiences! When he began, the only bandstand was a small box in the old Montpellier Garden and there were no fixed places for the band to play except at 7.30 in the morning when they assembled (in the small box) to encourage the water drinkers. Each day a different rendezvous was chosen for the band, so that visitors were unaware of it – Jones remembered that many times the band performed a complete programme for the edification of a few children and a nursemaid or two. A member of the orchestra recalled only too well the sorrows of the 7.30 band call. This was Arthur Wood, a flautist from Heckmondwike, subsequently a player at Bournemouth and Llandudno, who became famous as a London theatre conductor and the composer of *Three Dale Dances* and *My Native Heath*. He recalled that: 'The women had long skirts, huge busts, thin waists and marvellous hats with feathers. The men, silk hats and frock coats. I conducted [he was deputy conductor to J. Sidney Jones] in mittens – the poor chaps in the band, in top hats, blew their clarinets and cornets with running noses!' (He was paid £2 10*s* a week for four performances a day.)[1]

In 1895, however, bandstands were erected in the Valley Gardens and in the Victoria Avenue, the *al fresco* afternoon tea programmes in the Gardens becoming as popular as the evening performances in the Victoria Avenue. Still, there was nowhere under cover – in a Yorkshire summer! A new Winter

[1] *Light Music*: magazine of the Light Music Society. New Series, Vol. I, 1963–4.

Garden provided some relief but it was not until 1898 that the
Royal Spa concert rooms were opened, and the band was
expanded into an orchestra of forty-two players. Even then,
as Jones observed, an orchestra having to perform three or four
programmes daily could not give that attention to detail that
classical music required. All the same, music grew in popularity
and in takings. In 1900 the orchestra was relieved of its afternoon duty and its place taken by a large military band of about
thirty performers. Jones's orchestra expanded. Oddly enough,
at least in this era, the drums and triangle were played by a
woman, Miss D. B. Horsfield, who was in fact a granddaughter
of Jones himself; only in the last decade have there been women
timpanists, notably in the Hallé.

Jones introduced a series of symphony concerts on Wednesday morning which, despite municipal head-shaking, were
better attended than ordinary morning concerts. He also
initiated composers' nights on which appeared such celebrities
as Sir Alexander Mackenzie, Dr (later Sir Frederic) Cowen,
Edward German, Samuel Coleridge-Taylor and Hamish
MacCunn. Jones was, however, shrewd enough to mix his
programmes and to spice them with popular pieces, vocalists
and even humorous entertainers. After all, as Jones modestly
observed, he himself was 'more the carthorse musician than
the virtuoso', anxious to avoid inflicting on the public that for
which they had no taste whether it were popular or classical –
and, he added, the popular might be good and the classical
might be popular. Leafing through some of his symphony
programmes, one notices apart from Beethoven, Mendelssohn,
Schubert and Tchaikovsky, Berlioz's 'Harold in Italy' – at that
time by no means a popular composition – the symphonies of
the Danish composer, Niels Gade, whose works have now
almost entirely disappeared from concert programmes, a 'cello
concerto by Goltermann, and a violin concerto by de Bériot.

I mentioned that J. Sidney Jones had two claims to fame –
and the second is the more rare: he wrote his reminiscences.
I can recall no more than two or three of the spa and seaside
conductors who have done this. Jones's – though published
privately and bound up with the souvenir programme of his
farewell concert on 8 September 1902[1] – are fascinating, a
picaresque autobiography of a poor boy who never went to
school and could not read (except music) until he was sixteen,
a story that might be titled 'From fairground to concert hall,
tap-room to Tchaikovsky'. It reveals, often with Defoe-like
detail, an almost unknown side of Victorian musical life.

He begins:

> 'From street to tap-room, from tap-room to parlour, from
> tavern to tavern, from house to house, from the pavement of
> the town to the village green, from fair to fair, tramp! tramp!
> tramp! from morning to night. A hard life, you may say, for
> a child between eight and nine years of age.'

He did not agree. Born in 1838 and, as he says, without any
silver spoon, he never felt want because 'my little fiddle could
always procure me what I desired'. He slept on fairgrounds and
was befriended by gipsies whom he surprised by putting on
paper the dances they could only play by ear – and to prove
that he had done so playing them back to them.

With his violin he would visit public houses on the quayside
at Ipswich (where he was born) to see whether anyone required
his services. On one occasion he had been walking in the rain
and got wet through. At last he was called into a tavern where
dock men and sailors were making merry. Country dances and
hornpipes were what they wanted. Jones was swiftly lifted on
to a chair on top of a table out of the way of the dancers: 'The
merry making came to an end some time about midnight, but I

[1] Printed by Ackrill's of Harrogate.

was immovable with the exception of my arms. I could neither rise from my chair nor straighten my legs out, all my joints being set fast. Living a mile or two distant I was indeed in a fix, but no sooner had I acquainted one of these dock men with my circumstances than he had me up in his arms and carried me the whole of the way home. I had never seen the man before nor have I seen him since.'

Sometimes he would tramp from Ipswich to Woodbridge in Suffolk and then across the ferry and through sheep runs to play at a village inn for farm labourers and their sweethearts. There it would be four-handed reels danced by two couples:

One pair, facing each other, would dance out one strain of eight or sixteen bars while the other pair stood so as to allow the dancing couple to be in the centre. To change the centre couple a kind of S figure was gone through. This exercise lasted for about five minutes, when each person would pay me a penny; then another four were waiting and this amusement went on incessantly for five or six hours while I would take from twenty shillings to twenty-four shillings. The festivals lasted three days and I generally earned £2 10s; and was entertained free of charge by the landlord who used to treat me like a little prince. A very pleasant reminiscence of these occasions is that never do I remember one of these poor farm labourers ever trying to get away without paying his penny, which might easily have been done, as I was usually perched on a table.

When he was eleven he became leader of the band at the Colchester Theatre Royal, going on tour with companies. Then came an unforgettable experience: 'The first great work I heard given – with band and chorus was Haydn's "Creation" and never shall I forget the deep impression it made upon me, particularly the chorus "The Heavens Are Telling". When the basses ascended to the minor 7th on the tonic, just previous to the close, I felt my flesh creep and my blood run cold.' Alas for powerful first impressions: 'I soon found out that this musical device had become rather common among would-be composers and quickly got used to hearing this passage without this sensation.'

He practised with choral and orchestral societies; he helped brass bands, finding that the mechanical manipulation of the whole family of brass instruments could be mastered very swiftly. At the Oratorio Concerts at Colchester he would sometimes take the trumpet part upon the cornet. Some of the players were amateurs: 'I can remember taking second trumpet to the first of a dandy aristocrat, but unfortunately the different crooks puzzled him and (very much to his annoyance). While he was changing his crooks and trying to make out the music, I was playing his part by transposition on my unchanged instrument; he very nearly boxed my ears.'

During the Crimean War Jones joined the band of the Essex Rifles Militia and was promoted corporal. After the war he returned to Colchester, resumed his studies and taught small amateur bands. Again amateurs did not impress him: 'From what I can remember of these early amateur bands they were rather disappointing. All the violins wanted to be first fiddles, and all other instruments must be first of their respective kind. Each of the violins had an individuality which was very difficult to shake off; it was, "*I* play it this way, *you* can play it as you like" sort of thing with them.' And there were others: 'The one who could not tolerate anything below Wagner, which he understood about as much as a babe would understand Beethoven. I have always found that an artiste, whether amateur or professional, could appreciate the intricacies of Wagner, the simplicity of Mozart, or the voluptuous jingle of Strauss, all according to their merits.'

He set off for London with a fourpenny piece in his pocket and was engaged to play second cornet in the band at the

Cremorne Gardens. These Gardens – which lay towards World's End at the western end of the King's Road in Chelsea – were the last to carry on the tradition of Ranelagh and Vauxhall. Their focal point was a dancing platform upon which all classes of Victorians solemnly waltzed and polka'd in top hats and overcoats, Dolly Varden bonnets and Paisley shawls. Jones describes the scene at the Gardens on a Derby night, and mentions incidentally that Rivière (whose story has been told above) had just started his duties as conductor. Scores of sets of lancers or quadrilles were dotted all over the huge platform, with hundreds of others looking on amid the wildest merriment. Fireworks cracked and fizzed, and vast quantities of liquor were drunk – which was why, not long after, the Cremorne closed; in mid-Victorian times drunkenness in public tended to lead to rioting.

At nineteen Jones married, on a guinea a week. He became bandmaster to the Essex Rifles Militia – much to his surprise because, as he observes, nearly all the military bandmasters were then foreigners and Englishmen seldom had a chance. He applied for the bandmastership of the 5th Dragoon Guards, but since this was a regular regiment he had to enlist as a private soldier, being promoted on the second day to the rank of Sergeant and sent off to the Military Band Training School, Kneller Hall at Hounslow. Kneller Hall, founded some twelve years before Jones was there, was intended to raise the general standard of playing in the Army and also to ensure that more Englishmen should become bandmasters. It was still largely civilian-run, and it was not until 1865 that the Government took it over. Not all regiments supported it. Regimental bands, their instruments, music and uniform, were still entirely paid for by the officers themselves. Bandmasters ranked as 1st Class Staff Sergeants with an allowance of £100 a year from the band fund. (It was not until 1881 that bandmasters could be promoted Warrant Officers, and later still that they could qualify for commissioned ranks, the first to do so being Dan Godfrey's father.)

Jones graphically describes entering Kneller Hall:

> I was ushered into a kind of large classroom where some fifty or sixty lads were practising exercises and scales, every-one on his own account. Oh! what a din, what a pande-monium! And I had to sit down here and harmonize and score my examination paper. Well, I thought it quite im-possible, but after a few days I found I could sit right in the midst of the noise and not notice it. In fact I apparently only heard what I saw in my own work – a clear case of hearing with the eyes and seeing with the ear, a quality I always advise my pupils to cultivate.

After ten weeks Jones returned to his regiment a fully-fledged bandmaster (the present course lasts some two to three years for a bandmaster and some eighteen months for a bands-man). Of relations between bandmasters and officers, Jones observed that the place of a bandmaster in the Army was with the schoolmaster and regimental Sergeant-Major, somewhere between the commissioned and non-commissioned ranks. During his time social intercourse either above or below was not looked upon with favour, though good officers sought to break down the barrier. Nevertheless military etiquette pre-vented the bandmaster accepting invitations from the officers to join their social meetings; consequently he had to cultivate friends in civilian circles with whom he could feel on a footing of social equality.

Jones recalled that a civilian bandmaster, Signor Gassner of the 50th Regiment, an excellent musician and very highly cultivated as a linguist, was popular with the officers of his regiment and it had become an understood thing that he always joined them after band-playing on guest night. One

evening the General and his staff were dining at the Mess. The
General chanced to get into conversation with Mr Gassner and
became very interested in what he had to say. Later he asked
the Colonel the name and position of Gassner. After some few
days had passed the most severe reprimand from the Horse
Guards was received by the Colonel, requesting him in future
to keep his Mess 'more select'.

Not all officers had a deep knowledge of music. Jones tells
the story of an officer who seeing that the slides of the trombones were not pushed out and drawn in all together asked to
know why he could not get more uniformity. Jones tried to
explain that trombones usually played different parts: 'Oh
well,' says he, 'let them all play alike.'

With his regiment he visited Dublin when the troubles
between the English Government and the Irish rebels were at
their height. He was warned that at public concerts he should
not close with 'God Save the Queen' for fear of exacerbating
rebel feeling. The warning exacerbated *him*. At a concert in
the Rotunda he played the National Anthem not once but a
dozen times, merely, he says, because the audience exhibited
great disapproval. The more he played it the noisier grew the
disapprobation:

> The climax was a scene to remember, loyal ladies waving
> their handkerchiefs, gentlemen their hats, and the party
> styling themselves Irish Nationalists hooting. A few of the
> regiment's athletes and rough riders surrounded every exit
> while the excitement was at its height and as each disloyal
> person came to the door he was assisted out in a very un-
> ceremonious manner.

By now his family was increasing and needed a more settled
education than was possible with a peripatetic bandmaster
father. In 1878 his eldest son Sidney had obtained the post
of second clarinetist at the Spa in Harrogate. So Jones left

the Dragoon Guards, took on the bandmastership of the Leeds
Rifles – a militia regiment – established a school for music,
'The Yorkshire Training College', and began to coach some of
the Yorkshire brass bands, then at the height of their competitive fervour.

He became Musical Director to the Grand Theatre in Leeds,
a post he held for fourteen years, and which gave him splendid
material for his reminiscences. He describes (without naming
her) a 'Pantomime Boy' who of course was, and still is,
always played by a girl, in those days very often by a music hall
star:

She arrives at the theatre determined to boss the whole
show. Being a 'star', the producer has to bow before her.
She enters – a week or a fortnight before opening – and the
producer shows her the stage arrangements and dressing
rooms: 'What a wretched room,' she exclaims, 'and hot
pipes to warm it. Pipes do smell so. Smithkins (namely the
proprietor) told me they were well fitted. And I can't use
gas in my room, the fumes simply ruin my voice.' This is
probably the first and last intimation that she has a voice
and as she only confides this to the manager no one else
discovers it.

She then tackles the author, and puts him at his ease
directly by remarking, 'I think you've given me a rotten part'.
When the poor author tries to argue the matter, she rapidly
enumerates her scenes with such remarks as 'That's simply
piffle', 'I can't make these lines go', or 'an absurd situation
for a good song'. She changes her mind about one of her
songs and decides to sing another, so new lines must be
written to lead up to it; then she requires a clear stage for
another song, and so on. Should she think another artiste
has a song calculated to make a hit, she complains to the
management that they are giving her no chance at all and
so it is either cut or she sings it herself.

She next approaches the musical director to whom she is

perhaps more gracious than to anyone in the theatre, feeling conscious probably that he might easily 'queer her show', to use her own words. She hands out her band parts, which have generally done duty for an ordinary music hall band and are consequently incomplete for the theatre orchestra. The parts are often badly arranged and indistinctly written, so that when they are tried over, to an unintelligible mumble on her part they, of course, go wretchedly and the orchestra are blamed.

A 'bang' is wanted here, plenty of brass there (the parts contain one cornet and one trombone which may be sufficient in a small music hall but are decidedly thin in a large theatre), and some kind of vulgar noise at another place to accentuate some vulgarity in her business. None of these artistic effects are indicated in the parts. So the band is called for another rehearsal, a new song is brought which the orchestra have to try over many times until the artiste knows the melody thoroughly. Then she teaches the band how to perform it.

Two or three nights before the production she contracts some illness – probably a slight cold – and proclaims to everyone in loud tones, 'I am sure I shall not be able to open on Saturday, my dear'. This again shows her superiority by the anxious half-hourly enquiries concerning her health, and the numerous drinks sent to her.

For the pantomime comedian, Jones has much more time, even sympathy:

Everyone knows the man who, dressed as an old woman or as a fat boy, amuses the audience at pantomime time, but only those privileged few who are allowed 'behind the scenes' have seen him at rehearsal and in private life. (This comedian is the comic singer of the music hall stage, and no relation to the comedian of the theatrical boards.)

His favourite position in an ensemble scene is leaning against the proscenium, where he can easily arrange a little piece of business with the drums or bassoon, and should he be required near the centre of the stage, he invariably takes

1. *Llandudno Bay in the 1870s. By 1887 the former fishing village had grown into a fully-fledged resort with an orchestra of thirty-six under Jules Rivière*

2. *'Dr Malcolm Sargent – Musical Director and Conductor', from the Llandudno Pier Company's 1926 Prospectus. His reforms caused torchlight protest processions up and down the Great Orme. . . .*

3. *. . . and Dr Sargent a few years later when he had left Llandudno for greater things*

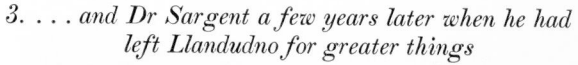

4. *The Kursaal, Harrogate, opened in 1903 by Sir Hubert Parry. To avoid any hint of the Teutonic, Kursaal became Royal Hall in 1914*

5. *J. Sidney Jones: itinerant fiddler, bandmaster, father of the composer of 'The Geisha' and 'San Toy', conductor of Harrogate Spa Orchestra for fifteen years. Portrait from souvenir programme of his fare-well concert, 1902*

6. *Horace Fellowes as deputy con-ductor of the Llandudno Pier Orchestra. In the 1930s he con-ducted the Buxton Spa Or-chestra*

off his hat holding the brim between his open hands and stands one leg bent and pointed toe. This seems to be his trade mark without which none is genuine. Should this comedian come on the stage at rehearsal with his hands in his pockets, then you know he is only going to speak his lines; but should he strike the attitude described, you can tell that his whole soul is in the part and he is going to show us how funny he can really be. He does not trouble the band to go through his songs until about the last rehearsal; such a proceeding would be giving his show away. Only humour him in his atrocious liberties as to time and tune, take his gags directed to the orchestra in good part, laugh at his chestnuts, and he is one of the easiest men in the world to get on with. He has a nod or an admiring smile for anyone of the band who has a prominent phrase to play, he will walk down to the bassoon corner and look over at the player in a most loving manner, and a whack on the big drum will make him flinch most comically.

He is indeed a jolly fellow both on and off the boards. He never wants to see the author for the simple reason that he intends to ignore him when he gets fairly before the foot-lights. His part then is nearly all gag; the author (particu-larly if he be a novice) will perhaps remonstrate with him, but he only answers, 'Well, my dear boy, I really cannot make your lines go. Let's go and have a nip and talk the matter over'. This generally ends all arguments.

In many cases he is a clever and well-read man – which you would never find out from his stage business. He is a most generous-hearted man, one of the first to head a subscription for an unfortunate artist, and always ready with his services for any charitable object. He never values his work from his own standpoint but takes the public's view of its worth. He generally takes a benefit at the end of the season, and then his liberal generosity knows no bounds; and if there be any part of the staff he looks after more than another it is the band.

And what of the musicians? The sharp-eyed conductor could scarcely omit them. One of his best *vignettes* is of the 'snob of the band'. He walkes into the band-room

> as if he was the owner of the place, addresses another member of the band, old enough to be his father, by his Christian name, adding some vulgar epithet. He makes his appearance in the orchestra and tries to make you think he is at least the leader (were it not for the instrument in his hands you might believe him nothing less than musical director); at last you are surprised to see him take a back seat with the second violins.
>
> During the preface of the programme he takes little notice of the conductor, his whole attention being apparently taken up with the ladies of the audience who, he thinks, are all admiring him. He asks his neighbour if he sees a certain lady looking at him. After locating her, his neighbour informs the snob, that this is his landlady to whom he had given a ticket. In no way disconcerted, the snob leaves the orchestra during the interval and mixes with the audience. A smile is on every lady's face as she encounters him, and he looks extremely happy. A moment later as he returns to the orchestra a brother member – who sat behind him and played the trick – follows him and detaches a ticket from the snob's back marked, 'This style two shillings and sixpence', and innocently asks, 'Did you know this was on your back?' The snob makes some unprintable remark condemning practical jokers, and goes back to his place in the orchestra quite satisfied that the ladies had *not* been smiling at his decoration.

There is a subtler sketch of what Jones calls the rare specimen of the amateur snob. Usually he is a pianist who can play some Chopin, a Grieg sonata or even a Liszt rhapsody:

> He walks around during an orchestral performance but never hears anything to admire. He picks everything to pieces to those in his company with such remarks as 'poor

stuff', 'wretched band'. If he sees a conductor, perhaps many years his senior, a man of long experience and one who probably has been progressing with the times, he then remarks 'out of date', 'committee should take my advice, then things would be very different', etc.

Poor Jones! He had certainly encountered this kind of 'know-all' – he might even have been a Harrogate councillor on the Entertainments Committee – for he goes on to say:

This species is a double-faced man, one who will meet the very conductor he condones with apparent goodwill, pump him, and then use the information thus gained to crush him if possible. This specimen is dangerous since if he is or is thought to be a good pianist, his words have great weight.

And then, of course, there are conductors – and conductors:

He writes in for a post which has been advertised, sends numerous testimonials which have been solicited from easy-going musicians. He is selected for the appointment, and goes to meet gentlemen of the committee specially got up for the occasion – kid gloves, top hat and frock coat. By his irresistible assurance he is engaged. He takes up his duties, meets his band, comes before his first audience, and now it is that we plainly see the man.

He surveys the audience, looks keenly round his men, pulls down his shirt cuffs, strokes his back hair, and then vigorously beats the desk for a start. During the course of the piece you will observe that he gives a prolonged 'hush' at all soft parts and throws himself at the drums for the loud. To conclude he scowls at the band, smiles at the audience, and wipes his perspiring forehead. Of course, all eyes are riveted on his excited gesticulations, many of the audience being so carried away by his antics that they wait in a kind of breathless awe for the grand climax; then is heard the murmur, 'What a splendid conductor'.

Beecham used to hiss for a *ppp*; I have seen Barbirolli throw
his diminutive self towards the tympani; I recall Sir Malcolm
wiping his brow. These are not necessarily signs of the charlatan. But they are not the habits of military bandmasters – and
J. Sidney Jones, for all his Berlioz and Beethoven, remained
a bandmaster to the end, as did Dan Godfrey at Bournemouth.

In 1902 J. Sidney Jones, then sixty-four, decided to retire
and at the end of the season on 8 September he gave a farewell
concert. What a night that was! The Harrogate Municipal
Orchestra was aided by the Harrogate Borough Band, the
Leeds Rifles Band, the Ladies Orchestra and the band of His
Majesty's Coldstream Guards under its conductor J. Mackenzie
Rogan. All the bands had played separately during the day
and in the evening joined together in a grand finale for Jones.
The concert is said to have taken place concurrently in the Spa
concert room and the Gardens; this must have been so since
the final item, the '1812' overture, was performed by over a
hundred players and they can scarcely have all been squashed
into the small concert room. Jones himself did not conduct that
evening.

The first item, by the Municipal Orchestra, was the overture
to Sir Alexander Mackenzie's *The Cricket on the Hearth*, with
the composer conducting. There was a humorous recital by
Mr Thornley Dodge, who sang an item by Paul Rubens called
'Algy's Simply Awf'ly Good at Algebra' and a song called
'Archie' from Monckton's *The Toreador*. Mr Nelson Jackson –
all artistes in those days got the 'Mister' – gave a humorous
sketch at the piano, Madame Adelina Burrelli whistled Luigi
Arditi's celebrated 'Il Bacio' and a Cossack dance by Tchakoff.
'The Dandy Fifth' by F. H. Gassaway was recited by Mr
Henry Marshall. The first part of the programme ended with a
selection from 'The Greek Slave' by Sidney Jones, Junior,

conducted by the composer, paying a return visit to Harrogate. Later one of Liszt's Hungarian Rhapsodies was played as a pianoforte solo followed by the first movement of Vieuxtemps's Violin Concerto in E.

Jones's farewell ended the first period of real municipal music in Harrogate. Changes were ahead. The Corporation spent £45,000 on building a new hall. In May, 1903 this – the Harrogate Kursaal – was officially opened by Sir Hubert Parry and there were two inaugural concerts. In the original conception the new hall was to have contained a spacious café, a smoking room, a billiards room, and 'all the accommodation of the best Continental Kursaals', including a roulette room. It was not to be: the cost, groaned the Corporation, was prohibitive, so the Kursaal became simply a large hall. *That* did not worry the *Musical Times* critic, who attended the opening concert. He was much more 'tempted to wish that a small portion of the £45,000 which had been spent upon it and on its marble columns, stained glass windows, crushed-strawberry hangings and sumptuous simulations of tapestries could have been devoted to increasing the strength of the band, which though very efficient is hardly large enough to permit of an effective balance between its various sections'.

At the opening concert Sir Hubert Parry conducted his own processional march from 'Hypatia'. The remaining orchestral items were conducted by C. L. Naylor, engaged as conductor of the Municipal Orchestra in the place of J. Sidney Jones. Cambridge-trained, Naylor was the son of a former York Minster organist and a brother of Dr E. W. Naylor who was well-known as the composer of a cantata, 'Arthur the King', and later an opera, 'The Angelus'. Naylor's first concert, with the orchestra augmented to fifty players, with singers and instrumental soloists, among them Clara Butt and Marie Hall, must have been inordinately long since it included the Leonora

Overture No. 3, the *William Tell* overture, six vocal items and four violin solos, Tchaikovsky's Sixth Symphony, Liszt's E flat Piano Concerto, and two overtures by Suppé and Auber.

Harrogate's season started at Easter and extended to September, October or even early November. Every afternoon and evening its Municipal Orchestra played in the Kursaal. On Wednesday afternoons there were symphony concerts (the orchestra at its full strength of forty-two). It was Harrogate's hey-day as a resort. Of course there were carpers. Gordon Home, who wrote and illustrated a book called *The Yorkshire Dales and Fells* published in 1906, was nauseated:

> Walking or being pulled in bath chairs along the carefully made paths are all sorts and conditions of invalids, and interspersed among them are numbers of people who, if they have any ailments curable by the waters are either in very advanced stages of convalescence or are extremely expert in hiding any traces of ill-health. . . .
>
> A white haired and withered man, having the stamp of a military life in his still erect bearing paces slowly by; then come two elaborately dressed men of perhaps twenty-five. They wear brown suits and patent boots, and their bowler hats are pressed down on the backs of their heads. Then nursemaids with perambulators pass, followed by a lady in expensive garments who talks volubly to her two pretty daughters.

At least he did not object to the music:

> When we have tired of the pavements and the people, we bid farewell to them without much regret, being in a mood for simplicity and solitude, and go away towards Wharfedale with the pleasant tune that a band was playing still to remind us for a time of the scenes that we have left behind.

Others thought Harrogate heaven, a place of perfection, of Georgian houses street upon street of them – as A. A. Thomson put it in his autobiographical novel *The Exquisite Burden* –

ringed about by green, inviolable spaces that could never be built on or desecrated. A town of broughams and landaus and, of course, bath-chairs, its residential population containing a bare minimum of working inhabitants, no slums and only two poor streets. A town of many old ladies who spent the whole summer there and were a race apart – very stout, very kindly and very rich. Usually they were seen in carriages not going anywhere in particular but just for a drive and sometimes they were to be seen being towed up the steep walks by bent bath-chair men. Harrogate had its aristocratic and distinguished clients, too; it has been said that so many eminent statesmen were among them that at the height of Queen Victoria's reign she could have held a Cabinet meeting there in the season.

And they all listened to the band. In the evening they strolled down to the Kursaal in their frilly Edwardian dinner jackets with good claret and port beneath their waistcoats, and their ladies on their arms. Perhaps they did not know or care much about music; perhaps they did not notice the departure in 1906 of the austere maestro, Naylor, hymn writer and editor of the Methodist school hymnal. Happier in the organ loft than on the podium, less happy still in controlling musicians who, like medical students, have always been known for their crude jokes and their tendency to be disrespectful, he happily made way for – a phenomenon.

The phenomenon was called Julian Clifford. Tall, slim, with wavy hair carefully parted on the right and sufficient left at the back to establish that he was indeed an artist, he belonged to the comparatively new race of virtuoso conductors. He descended more from the Julliens and the Rivières than from the Hallés and the Manns. Not that he lacked a thorough musical education. Though sprung from the landed gentry, the son of Thomas Clifford of Dryhill Park, near Tonbridge in Kent, and educated at Ardingly College and Tonbridge School, he

had studied at the Leipzig Conservatory and the Royal College
of Music. By the time he was fifteen he was organist and choirmaster at the English Church in Leipzig. He had been solo
pianist at London concerts, and was a composer of merit, his
piano concerto – which incidentally Sir Dan Godfrey scored
for orchestra – being quite frequently played in the early years
of the twentieth century. He wrote an Ode to the New Year, an
orchestral ballad, a tone poem 'Lights Out' and a song cycle
'The Dream of Flowers'. He had married within his class – the
elder daughter of the 5th Lord Henniker, who at one time was
Governor of the Isle of Man; but the Hon. Mrs Julian Clifford
was a trained singer and before their arrival at Harrogate she
toured with her husband giving recitals and concerts at such
places as Buxton and Bath.

Clifford was one of the early showman conductors – and
what English music needed at the time was showmen, people
who by their personality could gain a great following, for only
such *maestros* could successfully launch the new music at last
being written by English composers – or for that matter un-
fashionable old music. From them the public would take
anything, however unfamiliar and bizarre – just as they would
take and applaud Delius and Sibelius from Beecham if from
no one else. Perhaps with the classics Julian Clifford was less
than top class. His friend Sir Dan Godfrey wrote: 'As a
conductor, he always seemed to me to be too imitative in his
interpretations to be considered great. His reading savoured
too much of superficial effect and too little of real inspiration,
with the result that they seemed to be the ideas which he had
culled from other people.'

But Godfrey did not doubt his contribution to municipal
music and his help to young British composers. As is the case
with Godfrey himself, many of these new British compositions
are now totally forgotten. Clifford for example, as well as

claiming the distinction of giving the first provincial performance of Elgar's Second Symphony on 9 August 1911, produced
new works by such people as George Boyle, Ernest Farrar –
whose death in action in 1918 at the age of thirty-three was
regarded as a serious loss to British music – and many others
whose forgotten names are listed at the end of Sir Dan Godfrey's
own memoirs.

Clifford's music was celebrated far beyond the immediate
vicinity of Harrogate, and he formed the Yorkshire Permanent
Orchestra which gave symphony concerts all over the Northern
counties. At one time he took the Harrogate Municipal
Orchestra on tour round the British Isles with considerable
success. His symphony concerts included fewer and fewer of
the purely vocal items which had been regarded as essential
in earlier days. Nevertheless he invited the world's greatest
artists to Harrogate: Kreisler, Melba, Tetrazzini, Busoni,
Paderewski, Ysaÿe and Elman all visited the Kursaal. And
Clifford, being general entertainments manager as well as
musical director in Harrogate, occupied a key position in the
development of the spa in those years.

He had some of the failings of the virtuoso – the over-flashy
style, the over-ornate stock, the showy gesture (how often did
he throw himself at the timpani?). Too often, he presented
Mrs Julian Clifford singing Arditi's 'Il Bacio'; he would have
been well advised not to introduce his son, Julian, aged four,
as the youngest conductor in the world – he directed the
orchestra in Sousa's 'Invincible Eagle' march and 'The Teddy
Bears' Picnic' by Bratten. (This Julian Clifford II subsequently
played the drums and studied at the Royal College of Music.
Between the wars he conducted various orchestras and did
much work for the B.B.C.)

The 1914 war in no way abated Harrogate's musical life; in
fact its attractions as a resort increased, since many who had

been in the habit of visiting Austria and France now had to satisfy themselves with the home product. Wagner was still played; so too were the new works of Delius. But the Kursaal, to avoid any suggestion of the Teutonic, became instead the Royal Hall, the name it bears today. Despite this, on 9 October 1914, a Clifford benefit, there was shown at the end of the afternoon concert 'the wonderful film *Tannhäuser*' which had music – from the pit not the screen – arranged by Ernest Farrar and Julian Clifford.

How inexpensive music was before 1914! For the twenty-six weekly symphony concerts of the 1912 season, for example, half a guinea secured a season ticket for admission to the main body of the hall and to the upper circle, while for a guinea one could sit in the best seats in the house – at a cost of less than tenpence a concert. These prices continued throughout the war. In February 1915, the Corporation gave Clifford £3,500 a year to spend on the orchestras in the Crescent Gardens and the Royal Hall. No profit was made from the provision of music; this did not matter because the odd belief persisted that it was as reasonable to spend money on orchestras to draw visitors as it was to spend money on ornamental gardens, promenades and other amenities. The belief scarcely outlasted the decade.

The war over, there was a promising new development. Before 1919 the Harrogate Municipal Orchestra played from Easter to October and was then disbanded until the next Easter. But in 1919 Hastings decided to have a municipal orchestra. There the requirement was for a winter orchestra. What more natural than that Clifford's orchestra should move to Hastings in the autumn, returning to Harrogate at Easter? It had also the advantage of keeping the players together. This dovetailing lasted until 1930.

Julian Clifford died at the age of forty-four in 1921 and was mourned throughout the musical world, not least in Harrogate. He was buried at St Leonards and his orchestra played at the funeral under the direction of Sir Dan Godfrey.

Clifford's death marked the end of an epoch in Harrogate. The war over, the aristocracy and the gentry, already somewhat reduced in numbers, sought replenishment of their vital powers further afield than the English resorts; Harrogate became almost exclusively a middle-class holiday centre. The old were in greater numbers than ever and, although the waters were still drunk, the drinking became less of a ritual occasion. The drinkers still required some music to help down the sulphurous brew; and as late as 1939 the road between the Pump Room and Parliament Street was closed to traffic from 8 a.m. to 10 a.m. so that drinkers could sit at ease at small tables under striped umbrellas and listen to the band – while the landaus and the bath-chairs and their attendants waited at the top of Montpellier Parade.

All the same, tastes were changing: cinemas with organs, the dancing craze and Negro Jazz, Berg, Schönberg, Hindemith were on their way. So were the gramophone and the wireless. As yet all these were distantly heard in Harrogate but together they would eventually devastate the old order even in that 'Northern Spaw'. And the great economic depression would speed the devastation.

In 1921 when Clifford died Harrogate had no thought of such things. The immediate problem was to find a successor, if possible with the attributes of the late *maestro*. The choice fell on Howard Carr, most of whose experience had been in theatres, as assistant at the Covent Garden Opera in London and as a touring conductor of light opera. He was a composer both of orchestral and lighter works – including the successful musical comedy *The Chinese Honeymoon* – and some of the former were produced at the Promenade concerts.[1] Carr was an adept arranger of music and many years later did the orchestrations and arrangements for the B.B.C. Theatre Orchestra. One of his arrangements was of the music which Respighi orchestrated from pieces by Rossini for Massine's ballet 'La Boutique Fantasque'. In Carr's arrangement this was played by resort orchestras all over the country in between the wars. But perhaps because of his less ebullient style as a conductor he did not click with Harrogate, though he began a series of instructional concerts for school children in the area and founded a municipal choir. He resigned after only two years – because, it was said, he refused to include jazz in his programmes.

His successor was Basil Cameron, a distinguished musician still alive, who has conducted most of the great orchestras of the world and latterly was associate conductor of the Promenade concerts with the late Sir Malcolm Sargent. Cameron, trained in music in Berlin, first came to notice as a conductor at Torquay in 1912, where he founded the municipal orchestra with twenty-five players. He was deeply interested in the upper stratum of music and more particularly in German music. When he went to Torquay he believed that no musician with such an English or perhaps Scottish name as his own could succeed, and he therefore adopted his mother's maiden name, which was Hindenburg, first appearing before the public as George Basil Hindenburg. He held Wagner festivals and concerts devoted to the music of Richard Strauss, then still a rather advanced composer. For these festivals his orchestra

---

[1] Carr composed an orchestral work with all the period flavour of the First World War – 'Three Heroes', sketches for orchestra, produced at the Promenade Concerts and at Buxton in 1919. It was quite overshadowed later on by Bliss's much more elaborate *Morning Heroes*. Carr's three heroes were Lance-Corporal O'Leary v.c., Captain Oates of Scott's polar expedition and R. A. J. Warneford, v.c. who single-handed attacked and destroyed a Zeppelin in mid-air.

was augmented to seventy. But then the war came and with it
anti-German feeling. In one of the local Torquay newspapers
there were in 1914 two headlines almost alongside each other.
One read 'Hindenburg's Wagner Festival Great Success' and
the other 'Hindenburg Breaks Through the ... Line'. (The
missing word was of course censored). The orchestra itself did
not in fact survive the war and Cameron changed back to his
own name. A story was told that shortly after this in the
Savage Club Beecham asked him 'Hello Basil, what alias are
you trading under these days?' (This incidentally is Cameron's
own story.)

Cameron started in Harrogate with an orchestra of some
thirty-three permanent members which gave concerts daily
throughout the summer season at the Royal Hall and was
enlarged each Wednesday evening for the weekly symphony
concert. Cameron was much more a real orchestral trainer
than any of his predecessors, and under his guidance the
municipal orchestra in Harrogate became first-class. He
presented all kinds of new music, both British and Continental.
At the three-day festival in 1927 he gave the first English
performance of Malipiero's Symphonic Fragments from the
oratorio *San Francesco d'Assisi* (1920), and new works by
Victor Hely-Hutchinson, Norman O'Neill and Elgar. At a
later, all-British festival in 1929 he presented compositions by
Delius, Bax, Peter Warlock, Balfour Gardiner, Holbrooke,
Hurlstone and again Norman O'Neill.

One of the composers Cameron introduced to Harrogate was
Eric Coates. Coates had brought a new, lively and very
musicianly element into light music. He had been a colleague of
Cameron before the war when Cameron played his violin and
Coates his viola in the Queen's Hall Orchestra (along with
Eugene Goossens, John Barbirolli, and many other sub-
sequently well-known musicians.) In his memoirs Coates has

some amusing stories to tell about Cameron and himself in those days when both were longing to break away from the grind of orchestral playing under Henry Wood. Coates remembered 'one fantastic afternoon when we [i.e. Cameron and himself] hired a hansom during a stay in Norwich where we were playing in the festival, and between rehearsal and concert went for a wild ride into the country. We both leaned out over the doors of the cab and made faces at every person who hove in sight, and every now and then Basil would emit an ear-splitting screech which caused the cabby to open the trap-door overhead to enquire if we were feeling all right'.

Now twenty years later Cameron asked his old friend Coates to write a new work for the Harrogate festival. Coates, feeling lazy, replied that he could not think of anything. Cameron pressed him. Some weeks later Coates got a telegram saying that the musical director at Harrogate wished to know the title of the new work. Coates had not even begun. But suddenly an idea came to him and he replied by telegram 'New work "Four Ways". When must you have it? Not started yet'. It was ready just in time. At its first performance, an odd thing happened: half the audience rose and stood to attention. This was because in the first bars of the opening movement there was a side drum roll and a cymbal crash which somehow gave the impression that the National Anthem was to follow.

Basil Cameron was an excellent conductor, although some of his players jocosely criticised his action on the platform, saying that he always appeared to be trying to get out of a sack. But his programme planning was not attuned to resort requirements. His programmes tended to be too solid and to lack the light relief that the spa's audiences needed. Dan Godfrey was more guileful, as was Alick Maclean at Scarborough. In his book *Memories and Music*, Godfrey mentioned that Howard Carr resigned from Harrogate rather than play jazz and said that he personally was always willing to play such clever pieces as 'The Kitten on the Keys' (by Zez Confrey). It was only the superior person who condemned such pieces wholesale; the conductor who did not wish his concerts to be a financial failure had to cater for all classes.

Not that Cameron's concerts were ill attended. The season of 1925 was financially successful, receipts being £2,000 above those of the previous year. On the other hand Harrogate was spending some £12,000 a year on the bands which of course included military bands and such small combinations as those at the Spa Rooms in the morning. As the 1920s drew on, costs rose and receipts began to decline compared with those of the pre-war years. By 1928 the start of the orchestral season was deferred from Easter to Whitsuntide and its end was brought forward. The Royal Hall and all its various activities, including the summer orchestral concerts, showed a total loss over the seven years between 1924 to 1930 of nearly £29,000. The 1930 accounts revealed that while there was a profit of nearly £400 for the period from Easter to Whitsuntide when the hall was occupied by vocalists, concert parties, enter-tainers and so on, from Whitsuntide to the end of July, when the orchestra was functioning, there was a loss of over £1,100.

It was not, however, just a question of money. Voices in councils objected that the kind of music provided at Harrogate was only for snobs and, almost synonymous, the well-to-do. A letter in the *Harrogate Journal* on 12 December 1930 typifies this attitude:

In Harrogate the minority who appreciate orchestral music have had a wonderful time at the expense of the community for nearly thirty years, for here they have found a municipality willing to enforce payment by those who did not appreciate it. If they still desire this type of orchestra, they might well combine and pay for it themselves.

During the next few days [when the Council was to discuss abolishing the orchestra] we are likely to hear a great deal from this minority, for minorities are always keen and nearly always noisy. But do not let us over-estimate their importance by reason of the clamour. The orchestra must give way to a more popular type of music and entertainment.

Many disagreed violently, among them the distinguished musical critic of the *Yorkshire Post*, Dr Herbert Thompson, who asked angrily whether it was also proposed to abolish the Harrogate Municipal Art Gallery and the Valley Gardens upon which a great deal of money was spent without any direct pecuniary return.

The calamity was not to be averted. At the Council meeting it was revealed that the municipal orchestra had cost £3,917 in the previous year and that a salary of £597 had been paid to Cameron. Alderman Lambert Foster, who was chairman of the Royal Hall Committee, said that while the music had never been better than during the past year or two, they had made little or no 'progress' and in fact were declining in their appeal to the public. Possibly, he thought, they had not gone with the times and the changed conditions. Their entertainments had been of a similar character for the past twenty-eight years (presumably he meant that they had kept on playing Beethoven, Bach and Brahms). Perhaps they were in a rut and it might be as well to try something fresh. If something fresh was not successful then they could always revert to the old order of things and perhaps the absence of an orchestra for a year might add considerably to its future value. So, the municipal orchestra came to an end. Cameron himself had been released early in the season to take up the conductorship of the San Francisco Orchestra, but he had made it clear that this would allow him to return if required for the summer season. The voting for disbanding the orchestra had been seventeen to nine,

7. The 'phenomenon', Julian Clifford, senior and the Harrogate Municipal Symphony Orchestra, which he conducted for fifteen years, 1920

8. Orchestras played every season from 1704 to 1939 in the Pump Room, Bath, seen here in about 1880

9. Conductor Maurice Miles, with contralto Astra Desmond at Bath, 1939

10. *Arthur Wood: flautist with Harrogate, Llandudno and Bournemouth orchestras. Composed 'My Native Heath' and other works*

11. *Reginald King: pianist and composer who led small ensembles at Whitby, Bridlington and Scarborough*

and in 1932 a lingering desire to have a seasonal orchestra
resulted in the engagement of the Eastbourne Municipal
Orchestra under Captain H. G. Amers to play in the Crescent
Gardens, the Valley Gardens, and the Royal Hall. The
experiment was not renewed. Instead the Royal Hall had
concert parties, military bands, visiting musicians of varying
standards and, towards the end of the 1930s, a small orchestra,
called the municipal orchestra, under the direction of a
Merseyside violinist, Louis Cohen. Festivals were given once a
year by the Hallé.

The great days were over. Harrogate had become increasingly
a town of flowers, of splendid trees, of wide green spaces and
even its railway station had hanging flower-baskets along the
length of the platforms. But it was no longer a place where
music could be heard from one end of the town to the other, in
halls, bandstands and gardens. Soon the water-drinking
stopped, too – perhaps the pioneers of the spa had been right
in thinking that only the sweetness of their music could render
palatable their water. After the Second World War, the spa
became a National Health possession devoted mainly to the
treatment of rheumatism. It became a dormitory town, its
hotels entertaining conferences rather than connoisseurs of
Hygeia and Melpomene, and its open spaces silent except for
an occasional military band or transistor radios.

4. The Oldest:
Bath Pump Room Orchestra
1704–1939

Let the loud Trumpet sound,
Till the Roofs all around
The shrill Ecchos rebound
        Pope, *Ode for Music on St Cecilia's Day*

BEFORE the last war, Bath claimed that its Pump Room Orchestra was the oldest in Britain, having played continuously every season since 1704. Even earlier, in 1651, a 'Band of Musick' consisting of five players – viols and oboes – performed in the Orange Grove, the fashionable promenade at the east of the Abbey. So successful was it that some of the physicians asked the celebrated Beau Nash to allow the band to play in the Pump Room. Its strength was increased and so were attendances at the Pump Room: wine needs conversation for its proper *dégustation*, water needs music, as we have observed before. Only then does it become true, as the quotation from Pindar's Olympian Odes over the Pump Room door states, that 'Water is best'.

The Assembly Rooms had music, too. Thomas Linley (1733–95) was director of public concerts there, appointed by the elderly Beau Nash, and created a fine orchestra. Linley was an eminently successful composer for the stage, setting his son-in-law Sheridan's *The Duenna*, Gay's *The Beggar's Opera* and many other light works of the time to music. He was succeeded by the violinist and composer, Franz Lamotte, and then by the celebrated male soprano, Venanzio Rauzzini, who in 1781 became musical director at the New Assembly Rooms where he remained until his death thirty years later. In Bath he ran the concerts, taught singing and kept open house at his country villa in Perrymead. One of his visitors, in 1794, was Haydn who there wrote the round, 'Turk was a faithful dog and not a man'.

When Rauzzini died such was his fame in Bath that he was buried in the Abbey and a marble memorial slab was erected in the south-west corner reading:

Near this place rest the Remains of
VENANZIO RAUZZINI Native of Rome,
diftinguifhed as a Vocal Performer
on the Continent and in England,
whose Judicious Abilities for thirty Years
in conducting the Mufical Department of this City
amply gratified the applauding Public
and whofe ever gracious deportment
conciliated their zealous affection

This tributory memorial was erected
by his affectionate Pupils
ANNA SELINA STORACE and JOHN BRAHAM
prompted by their friendship
and grateful respect for Profefsional merit
and liberality of Sentiment.
He died April 8th 1810
Aged 62

Anna, or Nancy, Storace was a well-known soprano; although her voice had a rasp, she was a remarkable comic actress in opera and operetta. John Braham – by whom she had a son without benefit of clergy – was a renowned tenor who composed parts in operas and became so rich that he bought the London Colosseum and built the St James's Theatre, both unsuccessful speculations.

With what music did Rauzzini charm the burgesses of Bath and the visitors so elegant and fashionable? It would be fairly easy to speculate, but pointless since no programmes seem to have survived. All we do know is that 'the musical band at the pump-room' performed there each morning for twenty weeks of the year, gave a concert each Wednesday night at the New Assembly Rooms and received two hundred guineas for the season, apart presumably from benefits. Should the takings exceed two hundred guineas the surplus was to be used for further performances by the band at ten guineas a week. It is not clear how the money was divided nor among how many. Perhaps this was the cause of trouble in 1783 when a visitor enquiring one morning why there was no music in the Pump Room – 'the most pleasing of all entertainments to a refined mind' – was told that 'the man who provided the music [presumably Rauzzini] had had some dispute with the musicians so they stopped playing'.

The dispute was brief for the music went on under various

leaders, one being J. H. MacFarlane. Liszt came as a guest performer, so later did Hallé, Johann Strauss the elder and Arthur Sullivan. Hallé had been approached in 1848 to settle in Bath. In the end he chose Manchester but it is pleasing to speculate on 'the Hallé Orchestra of Bath'. Other visitors included Signor Rivolta who 'displayed his extraordinary talent of Playing on a whole Band of Music at Once without any assistance', and the American Slave Troupe and Brass Band, composed of freed slaves, who gave two concerts in May 1867. The German band craze began and the 'Hungarian Band Committee' engaged Herr Bartels to perform in the Victoria Park and Sydney Gardens. And – a curious note – in 1852 the Mayor offered cheap concerts in the Guildhall 'for the working classes': Bath was not all gouty burgesses and rich playboys.

In 1869 the Corporation took control of the Pump Room Orchestra and the music flourished under Salmon, Van Praag and, from 1892 to 1910, Max Heymann, a fine violinist and an able conductor who had played under Sir August Manns at the Crystal Palace concerts. The music he provided with an orchestra of probably between twenty and twenty-four was on the whole of a light classical nature, though symphonies were given occasionally. Heymann died (by his own hand) in 1910 and the Corporation bought his scores and compositions for £100.

Frank H. Tapp, a Bath composer-conductor, followed him, and during the season, which began in September and ended in April, he played all Beethoven's nine symphonies, all Tchaikovsky's six symphonies, and many other symphonic works by Russian and French composers. He gave a special Liszt centenary concert, introducing the Dante Symphony and also presented the first performance in the West of England of Elgar's 'Enigma' Variations, Gustav Holst's Somerset Rhap-

sody, and even Arnold Schönberg's Five Orchestral Pieces
which must certainly have been the first time atonal music for
orchestra was given in the West Country. Tapp claimed indeed
that he conducted at least sixty symphonies a season. (All this
was before 1915). He also encouraged composers such as Stanford, German and Elgar to visit Bath to conduct their own
work, just as Tapp conducted his 'Tempest' Symphony at
Bournemouth in 1914.

Commenting on his programmes later, he said he had to play
the Beethoven symphonies because they were considered
the pivot round which everything else revolved. Yet,
Tchaikovsky was the best draw. Brahms's four symphonies
attracted a fair crowd although they were not very popular.
Dvorak's 'New World' Symphony was always welcome and so
was César Franck's Symphony in D. Thursday afternoon was
the appointed symphony day, Thursday evening being light
classical. Saturdays were always 'popular', with operatic
selections and light music generally, though there was not then
available as much light music as later, so that Monckton and
Talbot, Sidney Jones, Herman Finck and such works as
German's Welsh Rhapsody and Georges Enesco's Rumanian
Rhapsodies were staple fare. All this went down well, perhaps
because, as Tapp said, there was something 'homely, something
indefinably intimate' about the Bath concerts.

But alas for Frank Tapp, he had enemies who thought him
too much the autocrat, and G. Bainbridge Robinson was
appointed in his place. Tapp, however, was awarded a pension
of £68 15*s* a year. To leave him in a less sombre twilight,
there is an amusing story from the department of strange
coincidences. While he was Musical Director, Weingartner
appeared as guest conductor with two celebrated soloists –
Clara Butt and Carrie Tubb. All, of course, performing in the
Pump Room at Bath, with Tapp in attendance.

Robinson, appointed at £278 for the season, was a clarinettist and a good musician – he was to have considerable success later with the Margate orchestra[1] – and he helped to produce the excellent festivals of music which began in Bath at about this time. Soloists such as Moiseiwitsch, Albert Sammons, Agnes Nicholls (Lady Harty) and Edward Elgar performed. Chamber music was given by a string quartet. Like his predecessor, Robinson did not hesitate to augment his orchestra with local and often amateur players. He concentrated at the festivals mainly on works unlikely to receive performances in the normal concerts because of the sparse musical forces. There was for example César Franck's Symphonic Fragment 'The Redemption'; Charpentier's 'Impressions of Italy'; and, since the war had recently ended, a piece by J. H. Foulds, a player in the Hallé Orchestra who later wrote a Celtic Suite and other light music, called 'Hymne Héroique à la France'. The programme notes stated this was 'quite worthy of the composer of the more famous Celtic Suite'.

In 1920 Bath decided to economise and Bainbridge Robinson's contract was not renewed, the orchestra being cut down to a septet under the direction of Jan Hurst. Hurst himself was given more salary than Robinson, being paid £350 for a thirty-four-week autumn and winter season. He had a benefit concert each year, half the proceeds of which went to him and half to the septet. A military band was engaged for the summer and Bath, like Weston-super-Mare, for long had its own military band under a German called Schottler.

Hurst built up his septet into a small orchestra and became a favourite in Bath. His sympathies were wide and he was of a pleasant and amiable character. On the other hand he

---

[1] See Chapter 11.

introduced much unusual music – not always to everyone's satisfaction. One day the young Arthur Bliss conducted one of his own works. During the interval a peppery Victorian subscriber was encountered stumping up and down the corridor in a rage. Asked if he had enjoyed the concert, he replied, 'Well if that's Bliss, give me Hell'.

He was not, however, typical. Audiences in Bath differed from those elsewhere in being both more fashionable and on the whole more intelligent. They wanted novelties, even if only to be able to tell their friends how ghastly they thought them – but they were glad to be able to claim that they had suffered the *dernier cri*. It was a sort of snobbism, for it showed that though they were retired in Bath they were not cut off from intellectual society. And there was always the *ton*, such regular visitors as the Duke of Connaught (who came for the cure and was very fond of music), the Comtesse Marie van den Hurdel, a patron of music, and Royal visitors from Queen Anne onwards. Oh, yes, Bath in the early years of the twentieth century had a clientèle not quite like that of other spas.

What other resort would have put on *Bethlehem* by Rutland Boughton – the eccentric composer who lived at Glastonbury – or even his much better known *The Immortal Hour* (in costume)? Where else for 6*d* (in 1925) – or between 1*s* 2*d* and 3*s* 6*d* for symphony concerts – could be heard Saint-Saëns's, 'Variations on a Beethoven Theme' for two pianos, an Arensky Trio, the Raff Quintet for piano and strings, and a Quintet by the now seldom performed Jadassohn who lived between 1831 and 1902? Jan Hurst also played such oddities as a ballet suite called 'Transcendental' by the Swedish composer Einar Ralf, and the 7th Violin Concerto by Pierre Rode (1774–1830). One day with his leader, John Roberts, Hurst decided to give a performance of John Ireland's Violin Sonata in A (written in 1917 but still thought of as very advanced). As they entered the

Pump Room, the first person Hurst saw was Ireland himself. Hastily he asked whether Ireland would play the piano part – 'I was not too sure of it anyhow' Hurst says – and Ireland did.

Hurst's happiest days were in Bath. Like Tapp, he felt and responded to the intimacy of the Pump Room, the audience always quiet as mice and nobody speaking even between the items – it was, Hurst told me, like going into a Cathedral. Moreover the acoustics were such that his orchestra of fourteen or fifteen players sounded like a hundred. It was there on one occasion that Beecham conducted this orchestra of fifteen players in Borodin's Polovtsian Dances; as Hurst remarks it must have been the smallest orchestra Beecham ever did conduct. There, too, came the pianist Betty Humby, immensely popular in Bath, whom twenty years later Beecham married.

By the way, odd things happened whenever Hurst performed the symphony of the Franco-Belgian César Franck in Bath. The first time Hurst played the symphony an old lady dropped dead in the Pump Room. Months later, playing it for a second time, the 'cellist stumbled on his way to the platform and broke his leg. The third time someone drowned in the baths themselves. Hurst never played it again.

Despite this, Bath was a happy place, especially for Hurst who loved all music, and particularly chamber music (as did another of the resort conductors, Herbert Lodge). But what made Bath so congenial to Hurst was the presence of John Hatton, the Spa Director. Clever, cultivated, a gentleman, Hatton was all that a true musician could desire in the way of management; Hurst refers to him as 'the finest manager anybody ever had'. Hatton said – in 1926 – that the orchestra under Hurst was better than it had been in two hundred and twenty-two years. John Hatton – who arranged a festival of modern art to coincide with a festival of modern music – was indeed a pearl beyond price, happily still in this world.

At the end of each season Hurst played Haydn's 'Farewell' Symphony (No. 45 in F Sharp Minor) with all the stage effects that go with it. Before it began, the electric lights and the chandeliers were extinguished. Each musician was provided with a candle on his stand by which to read the score. In the last movement as each finished his part, he extinguished his candle and stole softly from the platform leaving the conductor alone: solemnly, he extinguished his own candle, and departed. The season was over.

Hurst left Bath in 1929 for an all-the-year-round post at Brighton – to his eternal regret.[1] After him, in 1929, came Edward Dunn, a Manchester man born in 1899 who had been trained at the Royal Manchester College of Music, a young enthusiast who had had some experience in the North and was generally regarded as a showman. Oddly enough he also wrote books on aesthetics. When Dunn took over in Bath – doubling with Buxton – he devised a 'popular' Monday night at which there were all sorts of stunts, even slapstick in the middle of a programme. On the other hand, he would explain the idea behind a symphony in short preliminary talks before playing it; these talks were said to be illuminating. In 1935 he was appointed conductor of the Durban Civic Orchestra.

Dunn was followed for one season only by Frank Gomez of Whitby[1] and then by Maurice Miles who academically was perhaps the most highly equipped musician ever to direct the resort orchestras. He is today a Professor of Conducting at the Royal Academy of Music. In Bath he had eighteen players and divided his time between the Pump Room and the Pavilion which had been opened in 1931. His programmes were extra-ordinarily varied. On Monday nights, which were still 'popular',

[1] See Chapter 11.

one of his orchestra would sing a new dance tune, solos and even Tiger Rag would be given. There were light classical programmes both in the Pump Room and in the Pavilion and on Wednesdays there were symphony concerts, including works by Elgar and Holst as well as the classical composers. Miles used to play his symphony concert twice in the same day – at three o'clock and at eight. He also instituted on Thursday evenings a promenade concert in the Pump Room at which 'old favourites' were advertised. On Saturday there were usually soloists such as the then popular Anne Ziegler, well-known for her operetta singing on the B.B.C. and elsewhere, and Arthur Fear, an excellent baritone of the period. Such singers as Elisabeth Schumann, the Lieder singer, gave recitals and prominent soloists such as Bratza were engaged to perform with the orchestra. It cannot be said that Miles's programmes were in any sense a new departure, though of course there were new works and sometimes he was able to slip in something by a young English composer, such as Christian Carpenter whose Suite for Strings was played at a Pump Room tea concert. Like his predecessor, he performed in the summer time at Buxton.

Miles and his orchestra were frequent broadcasters. An astounded Britain – in those days of enormous radio audiences – one day heard an announcer state: 'You will now hear a concert by the Bath Room Orchestra from Pump.'

Music at Bath effectively stopped in 1939 although Mozart Allan continued with a very small band in 1940. After the war, during which a basket of incendiary bombs burst over the city killing some four hundred people, music was not re-established on a permanent basis, although there is a trio playing in the morning in the Pump Room, thus tenuously preserving the two and a half centuries-old tradition.

The causes of the ending of seasonal orchestral music are

similar to those propounded elsewhere: musicians under the guidance of the Musicians' Union became more and more expensive, and there was constant criticism in the Council – probably more in the Council than in the town itself – asking why ratepayers' money should be spent merely to provide music for a few visitors and a few residents.

Other reasons were given by Frank Tapp in an article in *The Critic* in February 1951, some thirty-five years after he had ceased to conduct at the Pump Room. He pointed out that in the greatest days the Pump Room Orchestra had not been competing with the wireless, the films and with large visiting orchestras. There was a warm feeling of pride in having an orchestra of one's own. By the 1950s, he observes, everything had become more sensational and highly coloured. Conductors travelled with their orchestras by air to America or to Australia. Modern tastes required a much greater element of showmanship and much larger orchestras.

The only way, he thought, to make a Bath municipal orchestra a financial possibility in the 1950s would be to start a co-operative scheme with the municipal authorities of other nearby towns such as Swindon, Trowbridge, Frome and Taunton. Bath would remain the focal point but, Tapp noted, 'an *immense* variety of music would have to be provided to make it sufficiently interesting for public consumption. By doing this, the conductor would not have to appear too frequently in the same spot, which would create the danger of him becoming a mere human machine.'

In brief, Tapp thought, there was very little future for municipal music in Bath; and the years since he wrote his article in 1951 have proved the truth of this.

Bath, however, is not quite music-less. From 1955 onwards Yehudi Menuhin and his family were the leading lights in an annual summer festival, lasting about a fortnight, with music, opera, ballet and such gimmicks as orgies in the Baths, an exhibition of Lord Bath's pictures and a Victorian Picnic. The Bath Festival Orchestra – an *ad hoc* ensemble which has also made recordings – has concentrated on 18th-century music but has given, for example, the Michael Tippett *Fantasia Concertante*, Bartok's *Contrasts* and other later music. The playing whether in the Abbey, the Assembly Rooms or at Wells and Bristol has earned high praise – and a small grant from the City Council. It has also been termed locally a 'Festival of snobs for snobs'. The 1930s attitudes die hard, and it remains to be seen how the Festival prospers under the new direction which takes over in 1969.

The New Music Saloon at the Spa Scarborough.
From a Design of Sir Joseph Paxton.

5. Alick Maclean:
The 'God of Scarborough'

The instruments that snore like flies
Seem mourners of Time's obsequies.
The sun, a pulse's beat, inflates
And with the band coagulates.
Edith Sitwell, 'Minstrels'

ONE grey winter's day in the middle of the First World War in 1916 a new orchestra was having its first rehearsal in the Queen's Hall, London – and there were ructions. Called the New Queen's Hall Light Orchestra, it had fifty players from Henry J. Wood's larger force, and it had come into existence because William Boosey, the head of the well-known musical firm, who owned the Queen's Hall and was known universally as 'The Emperor', thought the addition of orchestral music might revive the old ballad concerts then declining in popularity.

But would the new orchestra ever give a concert? This first

rehearsal was later described by its principal viola player, a man with a sharp eye, a growing neuritis in his left arm and a future that was to bring him fame and fortune:

> Our conductor, in his vain attempts to get anything out of us in the nature of a rapid crescendo or a violent rubato or a lightning diminuendo, worked himself up into such a state of frenzy that he became completely incoherent. The scene was chaotic. None of us understood what he wanted. The more excited he became the more he bewildered us with his indescribable, monosyllabic outbursts.
>
> I remember how non-plussed I was by his hopeless attempts to describe to me the way in which he wanted me to phrase a particular solo passage, and I vividly recall my equally hopeless efforts to understand what he meant, which resulted, after three or four play-overs, in my executing the passage exactly as I had played it in the first place and to my astonishment receiving a nod of commendation.

The sharp-eyed viola player was Eric Coates, the conductor Alexander Morvaren Maclean, better known as Alick Maclean, and his future might have been thought doubtful, particularly when we learn that he was sometimes referred to as the lightning conductor on account of the terrific speed he took anything which had a rapid tempo marking (it was said that he had only three tempi: quick – quicker – and damn quick).[1] In fact, Maclean was without doubt the finest of the musicians who devoted almost the whole of their careers to the resort orchestras. Coates himself later wrote of Maclean: 'Sometimes I think my dear old friend could have produced music out of a stone, so full of artistic feeling was he. His whole nature breathed music and with his music went a kindly lovable disposition which did not know the meaning of the word self.'

[1] It recalls the nineteenth-century musical critic who frostily observed that the only advantage of Sir Michael Costa's interpretations of Beethoven was that one could hear all the symphonies in one evening and still be in time for supper.

Maclean was no ordinary musician. Tall, high-shouldered and with a broad commanding face – in which the eyes had the inner-looking contemplation of the poet – he was a Celt, a kinsman of Sir Fitzroy Maclean, a nephew of Dr A. J. Maclean, once Primus of the Episcopal Church of Scotland. He was also an Old Etonian and one of the few conductors who could – though he never did – have claimed to have belonged to the upper classes. Not only was he educated at Eton but he was actually born there at the Red House during the time that his father was musical director. This father, too, was a man of infinite capacity. Himself educated at Shrewsbury and Exeter College, Oxford, Dr Charles Maclean had studied music under Ferdinand Hiller at Cologne and had an early career as a composer and organist in London; from 1871–5 – his son was born in 1872 – he was musical director to Eton College. But then Charles Maclean went off at a tangent and spent twenty-two years in India as a civil servant, and many of his son's school holidays from Eton were spent in Madras where his father was Inspector of Schools, Cantonment Magistrate, Supervisor Government Press, Small Cause Court Judge, Sub-Secretary Board of Revenue, Under-Secretary to the Government, and Government Translator in Tamil and Canarese. Later he was Judge and Collector in Chingleput, Madras, Nellore, Nilgiri and Salem districts. Wherever he went in India, he told Dan Godfrey, he was accompanied by a 'mile-long camp'. On his leaves, he was organist at the Crystal Palace. When finally he left India, he composed, and did important work for the International Musical Society whose publications he edited, becoming General Secretary in 1908. As though to mark the dichotomy in his career, his publications listed in *Who Was Who* include the Madras Manual of Administration in three volumes, and a History of Modern English Music in the Paris Encyclopaedia.

Young Maclean had a thorough grounding in music at Eton under Sir Joseph Barnby who had followed his father at the College as musical director. At first the young man thought he might become a singer but his voice was not strong enough and he took up the violin. He later said that this was not exactly a popular pursuit at Eton: 'When I was at Eton I played the violin. Well, of course, I was an absolute outcast, because I preferred playing my violin to playing cricket or football. I was put down as a harmless idiot.'

Nevertheless, in those days Etonians did not become *professional* musicians and Maclean found himself shortly after the age of eighteen a Second Lieutenant in the 4th Battalion of the Shropshire Light Infantry. He did not remain long in the Army and spent much of his time in composing – he remained basically a composer, in his own mind at any rate, throughout his career.

A very early work was a three-act comic opera called *Crichton*. When he was twenty he composed an opera *Quentin Durward* which had considerable success. In 1894 aged twenty-two he won the Moody-Manners[1] Prize of £100 for the best one-act opera by a British subject. *Petruccio*, based on Shakespeare's *The Taming of the Shrew*, was produced in June 1895 at Covent Garden and the composer received the £100 prize award from the celebrated Madame Patti. The *Musical Times* thought that *Petruccio* 'showed marked dramatic abilities'.

In 1899 Maclean – having discovered how hard it is to live by writing opera – became musical director to the theatres run by the actor-manager Sir Charles Wyndham, a post he kept for some thirteen years, sometimes conducting small concerts

---

[1] Charles Manners was an operatic basso cantante who married the operatic soprano Fanny Moody and established the Moody–Manners Opera Company which made extensive tours in the provinces, gave seasons at Covent Garden and at Drury Lane and offered prizes for the best operas produced by British composers.

before the play opened. *Quentin Durward* was given at the
Royalty Theatre in June, 1904. Its libretto – as in fact were
all his librettos – was written by his sister, who adopted the
nom de plume of Sheridan Ross. In 1906 Maclean's two-act
opera *The Hunchback* – German title *Die Liebesgeige* – was
presented at the Stadttheater at Mainz on Easter Sunday.
The composer was called before the curtain nine times and
presented with laurel wreaths.

The Mainz company produced it several times during the
season and, as Maclean long afterwards recalled, people there
said to him that 'they must be proud of you in England'.
Maclean laughed. The situation to him was ironical: 'They'd
never heard of me in England!' The same theatre some years
afterwards produced another of his operas with success – *The
Waldidyll*, based on a work by Erckmann-Chatrian. In 1909
his opera *Maitre Seiler* was given by the Moody-Manners
company at their seventh annual London season of grand
opera in English in the Lyric Theatre. The *Musical Times*
thought that it indicated that Maclean had uncommon power
as a writer for the stage.

Perhaps the most important of his compositions, the oratorio
'The Annunciation', was performed in 1909 at the Queen's
Hall by the London Symphony Orchestra and the then
celebrated Sheffield Musical Union trained by Sir Henry
Coward. Such highly-regarded soloists as Agnes Nicholls and
Gervase Elwes took part. Maclean himself conducted and was
'exceptionally good'. The Austro-Hungarian conductor, Hans
Richter, close colleague of Wagner and former director of the
Hallé Orchestra – the *Musical Times* referred to him as 'the
master conductor' – was at Queen's Hall that night and gave
Maclean high commendation.

Before writing further about the genius of Maclean, let us
go back a few years. Undoubtedly in retrospect music at
Scarborough was Maclean and Maclean was music at
Scarborough, but when he arrived at Scarborough in 1912
there had already been music at the Spa for some seventy years
of recorded time, and probably for long before that.

The waters, discovered by a Mrs Farrow at the foot of the
South Cliff, had attracted visitors from about 1626 – waters
with so nasty an acid taste that they were clearly meant for a
medicinal purpose. Their fame reached London, and there
followed a heated sparring match between doctors in Harrogate
and doctors in Scarborough over the comparative efficacy of
their waters. By 1777 Scarborough was well enough known for
Sheridan, the bonhomous Irishman, to write a play called *A
Trip to Scarborough*. In it Lord Foppington exclaims 'Strike
me dumb! Even the boors of this northern Spa have learnt the
respect due to a title.'

It was never, perhaps, so fashionable as Bath and Tunbridge
Wells or even Harrogate – the author of *Guide to Watering-
Places* published about 1826 remarks: 'The sons of pleasure
fly to more genial climes, and court the breezes of the south.'
A chill wind still regularly blows across its firm, fawn sands.
To augment its attractions a theatre was built – 'to the credit
of the company and inhabitants, a taste for the elegant
amusements of the stage is very prevalent here' – and three
circulating libraries were opened. Then in 1827 a company
was formed, first to build a bridge from the central part of
Scarborough down to the Spa and secondly to provide
amenities there. It was the Cliff Bridge Company who first
developed the Spa as an entertainment centre.

'Music at the saloon', where the waters were drunk, is
mentioned in 1840 as costing some £41 7s 6d a year. There
is reference to a band of eight performers. In 1846 there were

seven performers led by William Watson of the Prince's Theatre, London, an attempt to engage Jullien having failed. Next year the Leeds Temperance (brass) Band was engaged to play one month for £60. From 1849, a Mr Kohler, followed by a Mr Pritchard, followed by a Mr Williams provided the music, though not until 1865 is it referred to as 'the orchestra'.

By this time the old Gothic Hall had gone and the Spa Concert Hall had been built by Sir Joseph Paxton (the architect of the Crystal Palace), only to be totally destroyed by fire in 1876, when a westerly night wind fanned the flames and during the confusion 'roughs treated themselves to champagne which was purloined in armfuls'. The new buildings, designed by the London architect Thomas Verity and costing £77,000, were opened on 7 August 1879, when a performance of Haydn's 'Creation' was given to the largest concert audience ever assembled in Scarborough. There were balls and galas and the hotels were packed with Members of Parliament, Lord Mayors and Mayors of Yorkshire towns and cities and there was a sprinkling of peers. The Spa became the glittering cynosure of Northern eyes. More and more visitors arrived as the railway system developed. The Prince of Wales came and receipts leapt. During that year (1869) over 93,000 day tickets to the Spa were sold. Two years later the Prince returned with his wife, Princess Alexandra, and Scarborough's popularity was assured.

By the mid-1870s, the Spa was spending £1,500 a year on music, and at last the curtains open a little and from the shadows concealing all but the names of earlier musical directors steps a man with hair parted in the middle, a walrus moustache and a sweated look on him. Herr Wilhelm Meyer Lutz was destined to reign over the Spa Band for nearly thirty years, from 1867–98 (with a break of four years). He was forty-

five when he arrived in Scarborough with a wealth of experience
behind him – none of it, despite his German origin, in the field
of military music. Born in 1822 at Mannerstadt near Kissingen
in Germany he was trained in music by his father and settled in
England in 1848 first as organist in Birmingham and later at the
Roman Catholic Church in Leeds. He was a protégé of Cardinal
Manning and became organist and choirmaster at St George's
Roman Catholic Cathedral in London. There he composed
Masses. But he was also a theatre conductor, first at the Surrey
Theatre in London and later at the Gaiety where he composed
such successes as 'Little Jack Sheppard'. He wrote operas and
operettas, among them *Blonde and Brunette* and *Zaïda*, as well
as a cantata called 'Herne the Hunter' – all forgotten now,
though one slight work is still played from time to time, the
little dance tune known as 'Pas de Quatre'.

Lutz became an immensely popular figure. The young
Compton Mackenzie was presented to 'this genial elderly old
German' at Scarborough in the 1890s (by which time Lutz
sported a grey beard) and was impressed, he tells us in *My Life
and Times: Octave II, 1891-1900*, to hear that he was the
composer of 'Pas de Quatre' to 'which I had so often danced the
barn dance'. Nor was the *maestro* without a sense of humour.
Conducting what he calls 'a country orchestra' in Bradford
in the 1850s, he noticed that 'the clarionet player, a young but
clever and steady lad jumped about a good deal'. Lutz discovered that this was because his father, who played the
trombone, sat immediately behind him and from time to time
kicked his son, remarking 'Look out, Sammy, there be a flat
cummin'.'

Lutz remained at Scarborough until he was seventy-six and
died at over eighty in 1903. He was followed by a local organist
and conductor, Herbert W. Turner, who had directed the
'early season band'. There is a photograph in existence which

shows that the band at this time and indeed until 1912 was largely of a military composition, judging by the number of clarinets and of cornets and brass instruments held by the players. It was strengthened by a 'cello and a double bass; probably the clarinet players could turn their hands to violins and the cornet players to other instruments. Sometimes the Scarborough Rifles Volunteers band would combine with them.

Although H. W. Turner was paid £270 a year and enjoyed an occasional benefit concert, it appears he was driven to drink, for in October 1898 his employment abruptly ceased and he was asked to resign for 'inebriety'. He did resign, in a terse letter of thirteen words, and his employment was terminated with a payment of £10.

All the same, the Spa burgeoned and blossomed. Great names come and go – Sir Charles and Lady Hallé, Sarasate, Clara Schumann's pupil Fanny Davis, the eccentric Pachmann, Madame Albani. Melba appeared for one night; she was paid £250 with eighty per cent of the takings. Sir Frederic Cowen,[1] an all-purposes conductor of the time – but also a composer of very charming light music such as 'The Language of Flowers' – directed two festivals with an orchestra of sixty-five, and a chorus of a hundred and thirty-nine sopranos, seventy-seven contraltos, forty-two tenors and sixty-seven basses. He, however, complained of the sound of the waves and the howling wind – very disturbing, he thought, when a tenor was singing 'It is the sea, silent, majestical and slow'.

Sir Compton Mackenzie, quoted above, gives a vivid picture of the Spa of those days. He was there because the Spa had a theatre as well as a concert hall and his father and mother, Edward Compton and Virginia Bateman, often brought their company for seasons of repertory.

[1] See also Chapter 7.

We had round season tickets for the Spa Gardens, and what gardens they were for variety of interest, from the moment one went by the big Grand Hotel at the top of the cliff to pass through the gate on that side and go swinging down the wooded slope to the crowded promenade just above the beach. At this date it was the fashion for young people, even in their 20s, to walk up and down carrying a small ball attached to a length of elastic which was tossed ahead of one and caught on the elastic rebound. The promenade was fairly wide and ran the length of the theatre and the concert hall, by which it was bounded on the land side. On the other side it looked down over a parapet upon the great beach.

Alongside the theatre and concert hall was a narrow arcade with little shops where he bought bags of pop corn. Beyond the buildings the promenade widened for people to walk round the bandstand while the Spa Orchestra was playing. How 'thrilling' were the gala nights! 'I can see now the lamp-lighter going along the shrub-bordered paths to light one fairy lamp after another. When darkness fell we should have superb fireworks to gaze at with the added satisfaction of knowing that we should not be in bed until 10 o'clock at earliest.'

Meanwhile the band played on – but it seemed that it might have to rest on Sundays. One day a letter arrived at the Spa from the Blackpool Winter Gardens and Pavilion Company. How, Blackpool asked, had Scarborough avoided the attentions of the Lord's Day Observance Society? They themselves, though in possession of a special licence under the Public Health Act of 1890 allowing them to have sacred concerts on Sundays, were about to be hauled to court.

Scarborough had been blissfully unaware of the offence of charging people money to listen to sacred music on Sundays. Hastily they resolved to make the concerts free and advised Blackpool accordingly, only just in time, for shortly afterwards the Lord's Day Observance Society wrote pointing out the

criminal tendencies of the Scarborough Spa Company. The
Company took counsel's opinion. Counsel was very depressing;
he quoted an Act of George III that 'any place used for public
entertainment or amusement upon . . . the Lord's Day called
Sunday and to which persons shall be admitted by payment of
money shall be deemed a disorderly house or place'. Scared by
this, the Company ended their Sunday concerts: to be termed
'a disorderly house', even when presenting sacred music, was
no joke.

Courage, however, gradually flowed back. Cautiously the
company opened the grounds, free of charge, from three to five
on Sundays and collecting dishes were placed hopefully at the
gates for voluntary contributions towards the expenses, (about
£18 was taken on Sunday, 7 August 1892). Nothing untoward
happened so four years later audiences again had to pay for
Sunday afternoon concerts.

We watched H. W. Turner stagger unsteadily away from the
Spa. A successor was found in Charles George Godfrey, the
cousin of Mr Dan Godfrey at that time founding the great days
of music in Bournemouth. C. G. Godfrey, born in 1866, who
had been an organist, bandmaster to the Corps of Commissionaires, and conductor of the military band at the Crystal
Palace, came from the musical directorship at the Pavilion
Gardens in Buxton. His first appearance at Scarborough was
at Easter in 1899 and he remained there for ten years. Spa
music prospered greatly during his regime; while in 1907, for
example, £3,039 was expended on music there was a revenue
of £14,919 from the issue of 147,000 day tickets. Dividend to
the shareholders: £3,786. Godfrey left the Spa in 1909 to
become conductor of the Royal Parks Band in Hyde Park, a
post he retained until 1924, arranging music for military bands
and writing some orchestral pieces.

New furore! Who was to succeed? By now music at the Spa had become one of its leading attractions, even 'big business'. The band was still basically military but capable of producing strings when required. Its eighteen players were increased to thirty-four in August and September. The vacant post was advertised. Applications were to state salary required: in case an applicant heard nothing, 'Silence is a polite negative', the wording went. No less than seventy-nine persons applied, four were selected for interview, and young Lieutenant H. G. Amers, a man outstanding in the history of 'water music', was appointed. His band numbered between twenty and thirty-two, depending on the month of the season, and he was allowed from £87 to £120 to pay them, an average rate per player of £3.

But Amers, who was to do great things for music in Eastbourne, stayed only one season and in November 1910 Mr Charles H. Allan, whose small ensemble provided music in the winter, was engaged for the next season as conductor of the Company's band at £5 per week (or £10 when his band played twice or thrice daily). In a letter dated 19 November 1910, he assumes the Company will engage members of the band – previously the conductor had engaged them. Thus, he adds, – significantly? – the Company will 'know what you are paying for and it is your only safeguard against having cheap and inferior musicians thrust upon you . . . I will undertake to supply a nice smart uniform'.

Allan lasted only one season and the loss on the band was £133 19s 3d, despite the fact that the holiday town served the rich areas of the hinterland of the West Riding, of Northumberland and Newcastle, and of Scotland and Lancashire.

With such vast potential, music could not be allowed to flop. The Spa Company had its shareholders to think of. Once more, with a kind of desperation, the advertisements went out for what was now described as 'a musical director'. Once again

there were a large number of applicants, and the committee went
to London to hold interviews. There was a short-list of four.
One of the more colourful contenders was James Mackey
Glover – Glover being in fact his mother's name – universally
known as Jimmy Glover. An Irishman born in 1861, grandson
of a well-known Irish conductor and composer John William
Glover, he was conductor at Drury Lane theatre in London
and, as Sir Dan Godfrey says in his *Memories and Music*,
'probably the most famous of the stars in the firmament of
theatrical conducting'. Genial, witty, and of an enormous size –
Godfrey claims that he was the G. K. Chesterton of the
conducting world – he was a splendid raconteur and left behind
him two books *Jimmy Glover Hys Book* (1911) and *Jimmy
Glover's Friends* (1913).[1]

But Jimmy Glover was not what the Scarborough selectors
were looking for. Nor was another applicant, Arthur H. Wood,
referred to in Chapter 3 who soon after became conductor of
the Daly's Theatre Orchestra. Finally the Spa committee – it
was still until 1920 really a sub-committee of the Cliff Bridge
Company – plumped for Alick Maclean. There was really no
two ways about it: he was a gentleman; a composer in fields
other than dance music and ballads, and a man of commanding
presence able to dominate members of his orchestra. After all
as Joseph Bennett, the celebrated music critic, said in his
Forty Years of Music 1865–1905, 'These gentlemen did pretty
much as they liked, and in the matter of respect for, and
obedience to the wielder of the baton, they certainly could not
boast.' Maclean, too, had the indispensable *panache* to appeal
to varied audiences, as well as the highest recommendations
from – and what an extraordinary list this is! – Lord Roberts,

---

[1] An example of his style: writing of what he called 'this fleshy drama', i.e.
sex, he observes: 'The young bloods like it, the old bloods want it, and the
blue bloods even marry it.'

Sir Edward Elgar, Sir Charles Wyndham and Mr Louis N. Parker (Maclean had written incidental music to Parker's tragedy *The Jest* and an overture to the same author's *Mayflower*).

He was appointed for the season of 1912 at a salary of £450. A great era had begun.

Maclean's first band varied in number from twenty-one to thirty-six, according to the height of the season, and was dressed in black jackets and 'Gem' (or Homberg) hats, supplied by the Company. To fill in missing parts, the new conductor ordered a Mustel organ – the invention of a Frenchman, Victor Mustel – at a cost of £200. Two or sometimes three performances a day were given.

His first task, as he saw it, was to convince the Company that the band should be entirely orchestral in composition. It was not easy. He said later:

> When I first came, there was a military band. They had had nothing else from time immemorial, but the people tired of military bands and stopped away. I frightened everybody out of their lives by suggesting we should have an orchestra. They said we could not do it. It was bound to fail. But they tried it after much persuasion.
>
> The first day we played in the open was the worst possible. The sea was making a ghastly noise. My critics said 'There you are, you won't make a note heard', and they were perfectly right, for the opening piece began very softly and for the rest of the time the sea drowned us in noise.
>
> Luckily, however, it began to rain and we went inside. And there we met with tremendous enthusiasm.

The enthusiasm mounted throughout that first season in 1912. So did the confidence of the Cliff Bridge Company which even went so far, at Maclean's behest, as to countenance the building of a bigger bandstand. Designed by Sir Edwin Cooper, a native of Scarborough, it was an impressive oval-shaped white edifice with a golden dome and glass windows facing the sea, open towards the cliff. It was ready for the 1913 season.

As well as a gift for handling the Company, Maclean had remarkable flair for choosing players. His first leader was Alexander Cohen whose first public post it was. Cohen, a brilliant linguist who took a First Class Honours Degree in Modern Languages at Leeds University, had no professional musical training. Yet he was a superb violinist, as Maclean realised during an audition. He appointed him on the spot. Cohen stayed only one season. Later he founded the Alex Cohen Quartet which gave a series of exceptionally interesting concerts and broadcasts, always including in its programmes then unfamiliar works such as Hugo Wolf's early Quartets and the first Quartet by Ernest Bloch – indeed it is largely due to Cohen that Bloch became well-known in England. Despite this, Cohen never entirely gave up his literary studies and he became a highly-regarded translator of poems by Baudelaire and Mallarmé.

In his place Maclean chose Alfred Barker, one of the greatest orchestral leaders Britain ever had; he was later *chef d'orchestre* of the Hallé Orchestra and himself a summer conductor at Bridlington in the 1930s. Another early leader was Paul Beard, who subsequently led the B.B.C. Symphony Orchestra; he is still remembered in Scarborough for his delight in driving fast sports cars and his marriage to the then harbour master's daughter. David McCallum followed him – another leader whose capabilities were fully appreciated by Beecham and who happily is still entertaining audiences in the concert hall and on television. Later still came J. Andrew Cooper, a first-rate violinist for whom Maclean had a special affection.

One celebrity of the orchestra for many years was the harpist of the Hallé, Charles Collier, who was said to play like an angel. He had other less heavenly attributes, however. In the 1930s, a close observer of the programmes would note that items, such as 'Swan Lake', which included harp cadenzas always came in the second part. This dated from the evening when Collier enjoyed himself too much in the bar during the interval. Caught unprepared for his cadenza in the second half, he made a wild dive for the harp and fell though the strings, being extricated with great difficulty.

Looking at Maclean's pre-World War I programmes one notes such names as Mozart Allan, the 'cellist, and one of the finest players of the Scottish Orchestra, who remained with Maclean to the end; Stephen Whittaker, the oboist; Mendelssohn Fawcett who also remained with Maclean to the end as clarinettist and sub-conductor, and Otto Paersch, one of the great English horn players. Among others in these early seasons was Jan Hurst, who, as already mentioned, himself became a conductor of considerable style and experience of resort orchestras. This was Hurst's first job with an orchestra; he was paid £5 a week – in those days, he told me, riches indeed!

Maclean's orchestra continued to play each season throughout the First World War despite the bombardment of Scarborough by German warships in 1914. This bombardment was no slight affair and the Spa alone received some seventeen shells from two German battle cruisers, the sea wall, gas lamps, and panes of glass being smashed. But Maclean and his band played on, played so well indeed that it was rumoured that a certain musical U-boat commander would bring his vessel up under the Spa wall on warm, wartime summer evenings to listen.

Maclean's fame grew. But ought he to go on? Greater fame yet and certainly more money would come his way in London. The Spa urged him to stay and he wrote to the management: 'I am drawn towards continuing. I believe working together we can build up a reputation.' At last he hesitated no longer. Each winter from 1916–23 he had the New Queen's Hall Light Orchestra in London, but after that the Spa became his life's work. Soon there were people who visited Scarborough mainly because of his presence there in the summertime. Queues regularly formed outside the Spa Grand Hall, which seated about 1,500 people, an hour before the evening concert – for no seats were ever reservable.

Maclean became – quite unpremeditatedly – a character. He would turn round and stare at the audience grimly if there was too much noise, if two ladies were whispering or click-clicking their knitting needles. But he was in no sense obsessive about such things. He was perfectly aware that people went to his concerts on holiday and not as a general rule to listen very closely to what was played. Once he wrote a letter to the *Scarborough Evening News* saying that he had been much maligned: he did not mind his audiences reading, what he objected to was them reading aloud! Maclean had no intention of bullying his audiences: 'I would not destroy the friendly, intimate, informal atmosphere here. I would not stop them reading their papers or talking or walking. Oh, no!' In any case, he said, the Scarborough audiences were as well behaved generally as any conductor could wish. It was Maclean incidentally who taught his continually changing audiences that it was not proper to applaud at the end of each movement in a symphony; towards the end of his career this irritating habit had almost totally ceased.

Maclean brought many gifts to his work at Scarborough. He was a showman but he was a musicianly, well-bred showman. His heart and his being were in music. His performances seemed always fresh and spontaneous; even the old, hackneyed overtures took on a new life under his baton, Coates wrote, and he had a very wide musical sympathy. It is sometimes thought that musicians in the resort orchestras were bored with popular and light music and itched to be playing nothing but symphonic music, but it was never true at Scarborough. Whatever he conducted, Maclean upheld the high standards that his players were used to in the great orchestras during the winter. They were happy playing. Light music was performed with the same care as the classics, and exactly as it had been orchestrated by its composers, not served up in teashop arrangements. Several knowledgeable musicians (Eric Fenby, for instance) have gone on record as saying that some of the best performances of Mozart's symphonies they ever heard were given by Maclean. But he could, as Clifford Harker, the organist of Bristol Cathedral who sat under him in his early days, has remarked, make a trifling serenade sound enchanting. Equally he entered into the spirit of the latest tune of Irving Berlin – 'Let's Have Another Cup of Coffee', or a little piece by Cecil Lennox called 'Humming Along', or a selection from the musical comedy in vogue.

His programme construction was an art in itself; somehow or other he could hold his audiences with Berlioz's Fantastic Symphony followed by a popular piece of the time called 'Trees' by Rasbach – I quote from an actual programme of the 1930s – and end with a musical jigsaw. I do not believe that he much cared for the works of Ketelbey for example, but he had a love of Fletcher and Ansell, Grainger and Coates, for the waltzes of Gungl and Waldteufel, perhaps properly so since they were originally written for the bands at the German spas. He liked the music of Humperdinck and gave performances of Smetana's symphonic poems, particularly 'Vltava', which were as good as any to be heard anywhere. Coleridge-Taylor he often played and of course Edward German. He did not overplay Sullivan.

Here is a typical morning programme, that for Monday, 27 June 1932: a selection from the music of the Gaiety Theatre by Caryll and Monckton; Roger Quilter's Children's Overture; the 'Pastoral' Symphony; 'Will You Remember Vienna' from Sigmund Romberg's 'Vienna Nights' and Offenbach's overture to *Orpheus in the Underworld*. After the interval followed a selection from a musical comedy *Rio Rita*, a Fantasy on Songs by Wilfrid Sanderson, the Minuet by Paderewski, and the ballet suite 'Dance Revels' by Montague Phillips.

His morning repertoire included all the symphonies of Beethoven, of Tchaikovsky, and the better-known ones of Mozart. He does not seem to have included Brahms's symphonies in his programmes but he gave a regular account of the works of Saint-Saëns, of Ravel's 'Pavane pour une infante défunte', of Holst's St Paul's Suite and of various works of Liszt. One particular favourite he had was the newly-discovered symphony by Beethoven, now thought to be by J. F. Witts, called the 'Jena'. Those who may have doubted the authenticity of this work left the Spa believing that it was assuredly by Beethoven. Debussy, Wagner, and Borodin came into his purview, but no Delius or Walton; one criticism of him was that while his orchestra was admirably suited for the symphonies of Haydn, his repertoire of them included no more than four or five of the Salomon set.

In the 1920s he presented one complete symphony concert each week for the last eight weeks of the season on Thursdays or Fridays – it changed over the years. He later dropped this practice perhaps for reasons of economy – he took a cut of £100 in his own salary in the bad years of 1929 to 1931 – or more probably because he began to realise that his own normal formula was more suited to both audience and circumstance. He said once: 'I have always been a democratic musician. That was why I did away with classical concerts. I will not pander

12. *The Cliff Bridge Company's Band, Scarborough, 1893*

13. *'Beside the idle summer sea . . .' On the Spa, Scarborough, July 1919.*
The bandstand was designed by Sir Edwin Cooper

Left: *14. Paul Beard, leader of the Spa Orchestra, Scarborough, in the 1920s*

Right: *15. Jan Hurst: conductor at Blackpool, Bath, Brighton and Scarborough*

Left: *16. 'The God of Scarborough', Alick Maclean, conducting the scherzo of Beethoven's Symphony No. 7*

Right: *17. Basil Cameron: Torquay, Harrogate and Hastings*

to the humbugs who like to dress up and come down here and would like to force the rest of the audience to listen to symphony music all the time.'

No one who ever saw Maclean could suppose that there was anything of the charlatan about him despite his large broad-brimmed black hat which he had the height to carry. He never lost his Shropshire Light Infantry upright figure. When his band awaited him in the white and well-proportioned band-stand outside, he could be observed on his steady march towards it from the Spa offices at exactly one minute to eleven. If he was a few seconds in advance he would stop for a moment, take out his gold watch, look at it, look round and then resume his firm tread on to the platform where he was met by warm applause. In front of his music stand below the podium was placed a wooden armchair of the kind in which chairmen of companies used to sit. He would doff his hat, drop it into the chair, pick up his baton and begin – woe betide the dilatory! Sometimes in his latter years he would sit in this chair for a minute or so in between items, his eyes still withdrawn and occupied by music.

His platform method was distinctive. He stood with his right foot rather in front of his left and his beat was not the meticulous affair of, for example, Sir Henry Wood. It resembled more that of Beecham, if indeed Beecham's stick technique could strictly speaking be called a beat. Maclean would start off a work, particularly a classical work, by indicating the pace of a movement and to a degree this was then left to take care of itself. His points were made with the left hand rather than with the right, and indeed he had a particular habit of holding the stick vertically in his hand without motion to indicate that the time was as he wished it and that only the nuances were to be indicated with his left hand.

As with Beecham, much of the impulse came from the

G

movement of his whole body. Of course little of this would have
been effective without the top-class players who composed his
orchestra. All the same he was capable of the big gesture, the
large enthusiastic motion with stick and with eyes when the
music required it; and he had perhaps one of the most delicate
touches with the refined adagios of Bach and of Mozart. A
dancing movement was indicated by a dancing Maclean
although his feet scarcely altered their stance throughout an
item. He became rapt with the music and it was clear often that
when he turned round to acknowledge the applause he was still
far away from the bandstand or the Spa Grand Hall in
Scarborough.

He had a sense of the proprieties and when he played 'God
Save The King' at the end of the evening performance he
would turn to face the audience and raise his right arm and
with only a very few circumscribed motions go through the
anthem. He had no pomp though great dignity, but it was the
dignity of the music itself which filled him, as indeed it did
Beecham.

But if the music was often exquisite and usually excellent,
the setting was no less so. Maclean recognised this himself when
he remarked that the appeal 'lies in the open air club feeling
which music in the open and in the most beautiful surroundings
promotes. There was never a more beautiful spot, with its cliffs,
its sea, and the ever-changing colours of the sky and the
exquisite tints of the old town in the distance.' This was a
major part of the whole attraction of the Spa Orchestra. One
could approach the music from the Esplanade on the South
Cliff either by the water-operated cliff railway or, better, by a
number of gates leading into the gently sloping paths through
the woods and beautiful shrubs which had been planted over
the years. If the concert had already begun, enchanting wafts
of sound came up the cliff and one caught glimpses through

ALL MUSIC PLAYED BY THE SPA ORCHESTRA
TO BE HAD FROM

BANKS & SON,

MUSIC SELLERS.

AGENTS FOR COLUMBIA AND H.M.V.
GRAMOPHONES AND RECORDS

112, WESTBOROUGH,
SCARBOROUGH.

Cricket, Tennis, Golf, Badminton, Football,
Hockey, etc.

Large Stock.　　Best Makes.　　Minimum Prices.

C. J. Withnell & Sons
The Leather Bag and Sports Warehouse,
4, NEWBOROUGH STREET,
SCARBOROUGH.

Travelling Requisites of every description,
High-class Leather and Fancy Goods.

Est. 1859.　　　　　　　　　　　　Tel. 280.

Theatrical,
Commercial
and Press
Photographers

Wedding and
Outdoor
Groups
a speciality.

WALKERS STUDIOS

Telephone
146.

Studio
Hours:
9 a.m. to
8 p.m.

35a, St. Thomas
Street,
Scarborough.

ALL KODAK SUPPLIES.

The Hallmark of
DISTINCTIVE
PRINTING.

W. H. Smith & Son Ltd.,
31A, St. Nicholas Street,
Scarborough.

'Phone 91.　　Grams: "Gazette."

PROGRAMME OF MUSIC.

MONDAY, August 8th, 1932.
MORNING at 11.

1. WALTZ............Hydropathen............ *Gungl*
2. SYMPHONY No. 8 in F............ *Beethoven*
3. OVERTURE....The Barber of Seville........ *Rossini*
4. POPULAR DANCES....
    (a) I got Rhythm............ *Gershwin*
    (b) Journey's End (Casanova)....
         Strauss—Mackleben
5. SCENES from....The Mastersingers............ *Wagner*
   INTERVAL.
6. TWO FOX-TROTS from....Jack's the Boy....
    Vivian Ellis
7. (a) DANSE MACABRE .... *Saint-Saëns*
    (To the 'mind's eye,' Death—in this eerie and grotesque
    measure—is seen dancing by moonlight upon the tomb-
    stones of a deserted churchyard. Finally the weird illusion
    is dispelled by a cock-crow, announcing the dawn.)
    (b) PRELUDE........Le Déluge........ *Saint-Saëns*
         Violin—DAVID McCALLUM.
8. SELECTION........Die Fledermaus..... *Johann Strauss*
9. BY THE BLUE HAWAIIAN WATERS........ *Ketèlbey*

AFTERNOON at 3-30.
Light Syncopated Orchestra—Conducted by
RAMON NEWTON.

A WEEKLY Ticket for the SPA 6/-

ENTITLES YOU TO

14 Concerts by the FULL ORCHESTRA of 34,
　　　　　Conducted by ALICK MACLEAN.
(Gala Nights Excepted).

7 Concerts by RAMON NEWTON and his Light Syncopated Orchestra.

The HAVANA TRIO in the Cafés till 11 p.m. Commencing July 1st.

6d. REDUCTION to the Dances in the Ballroom.

A page from one of Scarborough's music programmes

the trees of the golden dome of the bandstand with its awnings out to prevent the players being dazzled by the sun. There was a choice of chair on the wide marble balcony, or below in the immediate arena of the bandstand itself. Everywhere was an air of total relaxation, only the occasional splash of a wave, the scrape of a chair to be heard above the music. Some visitors to the Spa preferred to stroll and then sit by the sea wall where the strains of the band ebbed and flowed but where they could observe the passing scene, the promenaders in their summery dresses, and in the evening certainly until the middle 1920s the men in their dinner jackets.

There was a true *douceur de vie* at the Spa in those years. This was music taken in the best and perhaps the most proper circumstances – not in a stuffy concert hall, with need to arrange transport to and from, the need to book in advance, the need to make a special effort to get there. This was music at the spring of which one could sip in comfort and calm and leave when one felt like leaving or stay to the end depending upon one's mood. Clean, bright, and fresh-smelling with the sea air, the Spa had its own chic and its own grace. Beneath the terraces, hung with baskets of flowers, were small, beautifully-kept shops showing the latest fashions, bijou knick-knacks, a ship in a bottle, hand-made chocolates. Picture postcards and crisply folded, excitingly smelling papers neatly lined up in racks were fixed to the windows of another shop; here, too, were the yellow-backed novels – the detective stories, the thrillers, the works of Richmal Crompton, P. G. Wodehouse, C. N. and A. M. Williamson, E. Phillips Oppenheim, 'Sapper', Edgar Wallace, Warwick Deeping.

Further along the Spa was a round-topped Pump Room encased in glass where until 1939 the waters could be drunk. In the corner café the Havana trio played for coffee and refreshments after the concert was over in the evening. In the comfortable Spa theatre, Greatrex Newman's 'refined and novel entertainment' called 'Will o' the Wisps' performed each evening at 8.15 and had a complete change of programme every Monday, Wednesday and Friday. Later it was Murray Ashford's 'The Bouquets', described on the programme as 'a bunch of refined personalities tied up with a ribbon of originality'. In the ballroom Hylton Cullerne, and later Ramon Newton, and Hal Swain played for a *thé dansant* each afternoon from 3.30 to 5.30 and in the evening from 8.30 to midnight when it was stated that evening dress was optional but desirable. New steps were demonstrated at 9.20 each evening and there was a hostess to whom patrons desiring partners could apply.

But the Spa at Scarborough was Maclean and Maclean was the Spa, whether he was performing his music in the noble bandstand with its two Ionic columns or in the Grand Hall on the podium with its half-circle rail, its deep steps and its fake-curtained proscenium arch at the back. He was, as one writer noted, the 'God of Scarborough', adding that though his actual position seems to have been conductor of the orchestra, nobody ever thought of him as a bandsman: 'The fervour with which Toscanini is regarded in Milan pales into insignificance besides the awe with which Mr Maclean was regarded in Scarborough. Devotees actually seemed to wilt in his presence, and the voices of small boys trembled as they humbly requested his signature. His orchestra was not an arrangement for providing background music to the waves. On the contrary, the waves always seem to have been excellently rehearsed as an unobtrusive chorus for him.'

Maclean was blessed throughout his career at Scarborough with an appreciative management which shared his own scale of values. He was respected as a man of honour, a gentleman whose word was his bond. To most of his players he appeared a benevolent despot, to a few a martinet; but those who had personal problems found him a true friend, as some have told me. He was neither self-seeking nor self-important. But he would have been less than human had he not been delighted when, at Christmas in 1920, the Scarborough Townsmen's Association organised a musical festival at which his works were the central feature. The Hallé Orchestra and the Sheffield Choir of one hundred voices conducted by Dr Henry Coward presented a concert performance of Maclean's opera *Quentin Durward* which by this time had been performed in London and in the provinces. Brief and melodious, the *Daily Telegraph* had said, there was not a dull bar in the score. The *Daily Express* had hoped that Maclean would give Britain the light opera for which Europe had been waiting long enough. The festival also presented concert scenes from Maclean's *The Hunchback of Cremona*, with the tenor Mischa-Leon and Hilda Blake as the soprano, and scenes from *The Annunciation.* Though the project was never repeated, whether because of financial difficulties or because Maclean's music was not in the end what the public really wanted, it was without question the zenith of his career as a composer. Maclean did not cease to compose. From his visits each year to the Continent and more particularly to Monte Carlo, he gained ideas for orchestral works which were performed in London but none of which attracted much public attention. Maclean incidentally never used his position at Scarborough to present his own works and in latter days the only composition of his own which he regularly gave was his adaptation of a violin work by Raff called 'Cavatina'.

But the fairest summer droops to autumn, all good things tend towards their ends, and as the 1930s grew on, the bright days of Alick Maclean were numbered. Still, C. T. Brock's fireworks showered the Spa in amber, coral and turquoise on Saturday nights; still the flowers bedecked the Rose Queen as she progressed along the Spa. Still, too, the trumpeter clambered into the wooded cliff side for the distant call in *Leonore No 3*, the band thumped out 'All the King's horses', or slid nostalgically into 'Artist's Life'. Emotionally vivid and susceptible as ever, by 1935 Maclean was showing signs of age. He was only just over sixty but in his season of 1935 there were those admirers who noted sadly that the maestro was taking increasingly long periods in the chair between the items. It was a surprise to no one when it was announced at the end of the 1935 season that he had been taken ill and that it might be necessary to have a substitute for the earlier part of his next season. Maclean was suffering from a cyst on his right shoulder, his conducting arm, and in London underwent an operation for its removal early in 1936. He never recovered from the effects of this and died of double pneumonia in May of that year. It was to have been celebrated as his silver jubilee as conductor of the Spa Orchestra; he was to have been knighted.

His death brought gloom and glowing tributes from all over the country, not least from the North. A year later after a memorial fund had been subscribed, Sir Richard Runciman Terry, for many years organist at Westminster Cathedral, and a very old friend of Maclean, unveiled on the Spa a bust of him designed by H. C. Fehr. The inscription reads 'Alexander Morvaren Maclean. Conductor and director of music at the Spa Scarborough from 1912 to 1935 inclusive. In his art – a genius. In honour – a true gentleman. In loyalty, courage and service – faithful unto death.' The words were more accurate than most funerary tributes. Sir Richard Terry said that Maclean could not help himself where music was concerned; he had to follow where his art led and he regarded music not so much as 'a career to be made but rather as a life to be lived'. It was part of himself. Although he had prospects of a distinguished career in other fields, the call of music was too strong and he threw over everything else to devote himself to that art:

> I always had the impression that the *doing* of his music meant more to him than any question of fame, or success as the world understands it today. I mean the world in which some of the Big Noises do not possess a tithe of Maclean's artistic equipment. To his generous temperament music was an end in itself, not a means towards the acquirement of riches. . . .

His old friend, Eric Coates – who each summer was invited by Maclean to conduct his own music – wrote:

> It is strange that Alick Maclean was never acclaimed as he should have been. I think this is mainly due to complete selflessness on his part, which caused him to take pleasure in bringing others forward to enjoy universal success that, through some trick of fate, he himself was denied. Alexander Morvaren Maclean. A grand musician with a great heart.

Of Maclean's final place in the pantheon of conductors it is difficult to speak, not least because so much must depend on memory. He broadcast frequently in his latter days and made a number of gramophone records with the New Queen's Hall Light Orchestra in the 1920s – some of these recordings are now collectors' pieces. From such scratchy evidence it is not easy to assess his qualities as a conductor. But his style, his *brio*, his artistry, combined with his Celtic fire and his English dignity, will remain always in the memory of those who strolled the Spa in his days and learned to love music behind his podium. When they, too, are extinguished in turn – pouf! the magic of Maclean twice daily exercised next to the lapping waves at the foot of the South Cliff in Scarborough will be gone for ever, no more than an entry in *Grove's Dictionary of Music and Musicians*, or the words of this present history by his erstwhile devotee in short trousers.

At least Maclean departed at the height of his glory; no chairman had mumbled in his financial beard about the cost, the out-of-dateness, the unfairness of the very existence of the Spa Orchestra – a minority cult – as had happened with lethal results in Harrogate and elsewhere. The only problem was to find a substitute for the 1936 season which should have been his jubilee.

The choice fell upon S. Kneale Kelley, a violinist who, after leaving the Royal College of Music, had joined the old B.B.C. Wireless Orchestra as leader, and had subsequently become conductor of a number of small municipal orchestras such as Broadstairs and Ramsgate. He had conducted the B.B.C. Theatre Orchestra and spent fourteen years in the service of the Corporation. In 1936 he had just been appointed musical director at Eastbourne for the winter period after the death of Capt. H. G. Amers. The B.B.C. and all connected with it had a great following during the 1930s, but the personality behind the microphone (there was virtually no television) did not necessarily cast the same spell on the public platform. In any case Maclean was irreplaceable. Kelley was a likeable enough man, a workmanlike director, an excellent journeyman musician. He inaugurated few changes – but even these the *habitués* opposed. One change was to open each concert with a signature tune which derived from the B.B.C. style of that time. Kelley chose the celebrated 'Ring Up The Curtain' from Leoncavallo's *I Pagliacci*. It set many of Maclean's devotees' teeth on edge.

The programmes played really differed little from those of his predecessor. Kelley, far from becoming more 'popular', set his face sternly against the simple dance tunes and ephemeral pieces that Maclean gaily offered. He reverted to the earlier custom, which Maclean had later dropped, of giving a symphony concert on one night a week towards the end of the summer season and engaged first-class solo artists. This resulted, however, in the rest of the concerts becoming more rigidly 'light', lacking the judicious mixture that Maclean stirred in his programmes of symphonies, foxtrots, ballet music and the latest hit from the musical comedy stage. Sometimes Kelley gave the first part of his morning programme to classical works and followed it by a second half, suitably titled, of music from the stage, music of spring or a music for dancing. Scarcely perceptible, yet somehow it was a decline from the great days.

With the outbreak of the Second War the orchestra was disbanded, but reformed in 1944, Kelley in the meantime having been conductor of the Buxton Municipal Orchestra. It started off in quite the old style with an orchestra of twenty-six which a year or two after the war was increased to thirty-one or thirty-two. Kelley still presented his symphony concerts and in other programmes extended the system of grouping music by title or subject, an attempt to meet the kind of competition presented by programmes on the B.B.C. In addition he engaged four permanent singers to take part in the evening programmes – in the old days a soloist had appeared for perhaps three evenings in the week and had then been replaced by another soloist.

But soon the destructive itch seized even the management of the Spa, Scarborough. They wanted something different and so probably, under the numbing influences of the loudspeaker, did audiences, for they were certainly down on the great years. At the end of the 1950 season Kelley was not asked to appear again; in the local newspapers some complained that no presentation had been made to him at the end of his time. Kelley himself, I have heard, was hurt and did not long survive.

In 1951 and 1952 with an orchestra reduced to about twenty players, the ubiquitous Jan Hurst was appointed and ably continued the tradition, though without singers and with much smaller forces. After 1952, with receipts still further down, the Spa Orchestra shuffled into disintegration, its place being taken by 'Grand Hotel' septets with such leaders as Tom Jenkins, or tinpan bands half-way between dance 'combos' and the later 'pop' groups. Sir Edwin Cooper's bandstand suffered the indignity of having large defensive screens added on both sides to protect audiences from sound or sight of the sea.

In 1956 the Scarborough Council purchased the Spa for £110,000 so that, after 131 years, it passed out of private ownership. Some eighty years of the lease still remained to run but the company could no longer produce enough revenue to pay national and local taxes and its shareholders as well.

The Spa today is a lacklustre relic.

A Symphony

6. Windiatts, Moggs and H. C. Burgess:
Weston-super-Mare

Who has not welcomed, even as we,
That jocund minstrel and his lays
Beside the idle summer sea
And in the vacant summer days!

W. E. Henley, from 'Bric-à-Brac' in *Poems* 1898

EVEN now as a dormitory for Bristol and a centre of aircraft production, it is not a big place, perhaps 45,000 in population. In mid-nineteenth century when it became Cardiff-over-the-Channel it was a mere village though it had grown in thirty years from 728 to 4,033. Yet Herr Deahl conducted his German band in the streets of Weston-super-Mare – a name it acquired in the fourteenth century – in the 1850s. The Italian Orpheus band, fifteen players, performed on the front between Worle Hill and Brean Down, looking out to the islands of Steep Holm and Flat Holm, in the 1870s, and was grievously criticised in November, 1880 as this letter from its leader testifies:

Weston-super-Mare. 27th Novembre 1880.
To the honourer Committee of the
Orpheus Italian Band.

I Leader of the Orpheus Italian Band I have take knowledge the your kind letter of the 21st instant just received
jesterday 25th, instant, sending to the band by the Committee, and find absurd the observations made from persons
not competent in Music matter, and who have not arriveid
yet to value the positive and indiscutable appreciations as
the selectness of the musical piece, some of them quite neu
and Classical, as for the innapuntable esecution and direction of those. In what who regard to the conduct, I do not
want to put in relief the education received in my native
countris with authentic prove, to have been serve in the
Italian army just in the 21st Regiment infantry, and I left
the Army with my perfectly conduct, with great displeasure
from my superiors, colleagues and inferioy.

Since the Committee, friends of the Band, find in the
Leader indolents unablety to his load, I respectfuly leave the
Committee to observe that the actual payment I have it is
very little for a Professor and Bandmaster like I am.

I knowing the realy provenience, or for beter say the
source, the origin of your kind letter insinuated from person,
although rich and Esquire, he is employ to me the lowest
social rank the which I not bold to mention it, in conclusion
of my present Protest it is to grant the Committee friends
of the band fourtnight notice begin in this moment they
have time to provide another Leader more able, more
educated, and more nicely dressing that is not the subsigne,

Nicolo Corrello [? Coviello]

P.S. I prevnt you since in this fourtnight notice it will take
place the second ball if (Bejcase) they have exigency of my
action it will be lend admist two ghinees, not five scillings,

with that money you can pay people worthy of the your appraising.

Dignifiedly bitter, as well as a bad speller, Signor Corrello (or Coviello) was followed by Corelli Windiatt's eleven (three of whom were called Windiatt), and in 1895 by Harry Mogg's military band, which lasted until 1953.

Mogg was a postman, also an expert clarinet player and for several years bandmaster of the Rifle Volunteer Corps. When he decided to form a town band, he mastered several other instruments and taught young people to play trombones, basses, cornets and clarinets. The band prospered greatly – many of its members were also called Mogg; in 1912 it won a Challenge Shield at the Crystal Palace.

In Weston, the band gave four concerts a week. One veteran remarked that in the days when the band started 'you either joined the Territorials or Mogg's band'. Another veteran, George Bray, said that he went to see Harry Mogg when he was eighteen. His first question was 'Do you know any music?'. Bray said he did not know a note so Mogg patted him on the shoulder and replied 'Good! That's how I like them.' Bray was set to learn the horn and Mogg insisted that he should never play a note without having the music in front of him because he did not care for people who thought they could play by ear.

In 1938 when the band still had fifteen years left of life, the *Musical Progress and Mail* wrote:

Here is the band's amazing record of service: Alderman Butt, President, 51 years; George Bray, horn player, 47 years; Fred Mogg, clarinet, brother of founder, 46 years; Frank Mogg, clarinet, son of founder, 34 years; Charlie Baker, conductor, 38 years; Charlie Rossiter, cornet player and band treasurer, 39 years; Jimmy Baker, cornet, 36 years; Charlie Slocombe, cornet, 28 years; George Cann, double B flat bass, 29 years; W. Lewis, horn, 18 years; Bert

Wilkins, clarinet, 26 years; Archie Wilkins, drums and effects, son of Bert Wilkins, 12 years; Donald Mogg, trombone, nephew of founder, 16 years; and last but not least the popular secretary Enoch Flower who was formerly a horn player but whose time is now occupied solely with his secretarial duties and who has 12 years' service.

Wonderful names, wonderful music, wonderful loyalty! By 1953 all had vanished. Under its constitution the band had to carry on as long as any six members were in favour. At a meeting early in 1953 eighteen members attended: not one raised his hand in favour of the band's continuance. Its assets were realised, its instruments, stands and music sold. The local paper bewailed its passing, ascribing it to the lure of dance bands, army bands and a 'couldn't care less' attitude.

During its hey-day, orchestras of a different kind had played on the Grand Pier, under Julian Kandt and Arnold Spiegler. Kandt, an Austrian, led a small ensemble playing in London during the winter at parties and functions, in the summer at Weston. Spiegler, a violinist and also an Austrian, played during the winter in a Manchester café opened by J. Lyons in about 1910. His engagement at Weston ended in 1914; leaving the town for ever, he cocked a snook at it through the open carriage window.

The war over, music burst out all over Weston: an orchestra played on the Grand Pier, another in the Knightstone Pavilion in the park, yet another in the theatre of the Grand Pier. Trios trilled away at Browns Cafe, Huntleys Cafe and at the Grand Atlantic Hotel – and there were concert parties at the Madeira Cove where the model railway now runs, in Grove Park and on the sands; the Carlton Fredricks Music Hall in the Boulevard had its pit band. The two cinemas had orchestras; Mogg thumped on; concerts were provided on Sunday evenings at the Odeon cinema under the direction of Mr William Johns.

But what music? This question haunts the *aficionado*. Doubtless it was often badly played, ill chosen, and under-rehearsed
music. A correspondent who played principal violin in a
Weston 'mis-called orchestra' in 1921 and 1922 tells me it
consisted of violins – augmented by the conductor's son in
knickers and uniform cap, one viola, 'cello and bass, one flute,
oboe, clarinet and bassoon. The brass was two cornets, one
horn and one trombone:

> We had a piano to fill in as best as it could the missing
> parts and the percussionist had a wonderful array of tymps,
> all the useful kitchen instruments and, figuring prominently
> on the bandstand, tubular bells. A total of nineteen includ-
> ing the conductor, or twenty if we include the boy.
>
> We were dressed in military scarlet with gilt braid and
> buttons and with this motley collection of instruments we
> played a programme three times a day and twice on Sundays,
> consisting of standard marches, Waldteufel and Strauss
> waltzes, Offenbach and Suppé overtures, musical-comedy
> selections and even selections from the best known operas.
> The combination was a contemporary music hall band before
> the invasion of saxophones and trumpet. . . . We were a cut
> above playing the pop music of the day which consisted of
> the arrangements just beginning to be put out by the
> Charing Cross Road music firms. We had to think of our
> public who, though they may never have heard of Stravinsky,
> had ideals and knew what they liked, in particular Albert
> W. Ketelbey.

This violinist, now with a London symphony orchestra,
recalls that with such small numbers the first necessity for a
violinist was to have a loud, piercing tone, quality was of less
importance: 'I certainly developed a very strident tone on the
very mediocre instrument which was all that I could afford in
those days. When I subsequently came to play in symphony
orchestras I had the greatest difficulty in producing a real

18. *Founded by Harry Mogg, a postman, Mogg's Military Band from Weston-super-Mare was champion British band in 1912–13*

19. *'The hall was as full of echoes as a gorge in the Atlas Mountains': Winter Gardens, Weston-super-Mare, with H. C. Burgess conducting*

20. 'Last blooming rose of the suffragette summer', Dame Ethel Smyth, who conducted her compositions at resort festivals

21. Sir Frederic Cowen: conducto and composer haunted by 'Th Better Land'

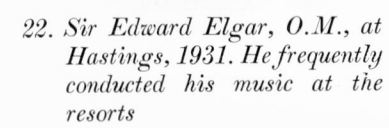

22. Sir Edward Elgar, O.M., at Hastings, 1931. He frequently conducted his music at the resorts

23. Eric Coates: favourite co poser-conductor of reso audiences

orchestral *pianissimo*. We also rather tended to rely on the brass to get us over any sticky passages in the string parts.' And he adds: 'The audience never seemed to know that anything was wrong.'

It was hard work, playing three times a day with only one session off a week. The average pay was £6 a week; my correspondent got an extra £1 because he was the principal violin. He notes, however, that the average weekly worker's wage was then £2 10*s* or £3 a week. There were also certain financial 'problems' of another kind; my correspondent discovered that the conductor, who supplied the band under contract, was receiving no less than £150 a week for supplying the band, the library and conducting. 'It did not take us long to add up our salaries and find out that he was netting over £50 for himself. Discontent was rife and certain action planned, but we had to stick to our contract and finish the season at the salary agreed on.'

But what status, what admiration was accorded to conductor and band! What side and swank they put on! The Sunday afternoon performance was a social event 'with all the land-ladies taking a brief respite, with the local tradespeople, with the visitors, sitting out in deckchairs in every available space while we played them selections from Gilbert and Sullivan and "In a Monastery Garden".'

The great event was the 'Sunday symphony concert'. Combining with another band and wearing dinner jackets, they were able – with the extra percussion player – to put on such works as Tchaikovsky's '1812' overture and Litolff's 'Robespierre' complete with clanking chains. As for the 'symphony', on at least three occasions during the season this note appeared in the programme: 'By special request we have substituted Schubert's "Unfinished" for the one advertised.' Perhaps it was the only symphony in the conductor's repertoire, and after all, holiday-makers come and go.

H   Y.M.G.D.

With this 'mis-called orchestra', Jimmy Glover from Drury Lane, whom we have met earlier in these pages, appeared as guest conductor. With him he brought his own arrangement of Suppé's Light Cavalry overture. The orchestra was mystified but he rallied them: 'Come on, you know this better than I do.' The audience loved it. An encore was demanded: 'What can we do?' he said to his leader, my correspondent: ' "In a Persian Market" had just been published and we had copies on the desk. I pointed this out to him and he said "all right". He had not met with it before and when the Oriental vocal noises emerged from the band, he said out of the side of his mouth to me "What's this you've let me in for?" '

All this is as embarrassing to think of as it was trashy to hear. Yet before the day of wireless and efficient gramophone, many felt an almost desperate need to hear music. 'Nowadays,' writes this former Weston performer, 'such a set-up and such performances would not be tolerated by people who have heard marvellous performances on radio, gramophone and television. Which is why, among other reasons, seaside bands nowadays are of the pop variety. Better a good pop band than a cutdown and fourth-rate symphony orchestra.'

Perhaps. Yet I think the seaside bands filled a need, and most of them played better things than 'In a Persian Market'.

In November 1919, a certain Harry C. Burgess, who had been wartime bandmaster of the 2/5 Durham Light Infantry, was on demobilisation holiday in Weston. The Weston Town Advertising Association, responsible for entertainments, asked him to supply an orchestra for the little concrete bandstand then being built at Madeira Cove. It was to play every morning, afternoon and evening (except Friday, mornings only, and Sunday, afternoons and evenings only). Its ten players would become twelve at Whitsuntide.

Burgess – who was to be the Master of Weston's Music for nearly twenty years – was the son of a Lancashire music teacher who taught him the violin and the piano. As a boy, however, he was a clerk-typist at 7*s* 6*d* a week; soon he was playing in the evenings – at £1 10*s* a week – at the Salford Hippodrome, the Crown Theatre in Eccles, the Hippodrome in Tonypandy, and just before the war at the Spa, Scarborough. Weston in 1920 was a great advance for him. Enlisting some of his Durham Light Infantry players, at £5 a week, he felt rich with £10 a week for himself, even though out of that he had to provide the scores. 'It was this last clause which nearly sank my ship!' he writes. The demands of eighteen programmes a week outran his own library's capacity, so from a former colleague he hired music for the season at £2 a week – 'already my £10 was beginning to wilt!'

After a few rehearsals at the old Assembly Rooms at Weston, the season began on Easter Monday at the Rozel bandstand, better known from its shape as the 'Dutch oven':

> It was a dreary morning and I still recall the misery of our hurried scamper along the promenade with instruments and music, in order to commence our first programme 'as advertised'! To add to one's misery, the library of music had been delayed on the railway, and we were compelled to play lots of music of which there were insufficient copies. So it proved to be not a very auspicious occasion.

The bandstand was so small that when the ten players were seated there was no room for the conductor. He stood outside on a wooden box. There were three performances a day – 'I hadn't the guts to fight for two' – and rehearsals were confined to the week before the season opened. But audiences were enthusiastic, life was good, and his heart was in it. Thumping out 'El Capitan', lingering over von Blon's 'Siziliette', swaying to 'Goodnight Vienna', the tall, lissom Burgess looked around with a keen eye. He noticed that no charge was made for listening to his programmes, his audiences consisting of people who had paid 2*d* to sit on a deck-chair; people on the wooden seats paid nothing at all. True, twice during each performance an odd character named Baillie shook a collecting box at the free seats, some of whom responded with coppers, others claiming exemption by muttering 'I am a rate-payer!' 'Often,' remarks Burgess, 'I would hear vocal effects not marked in my score.' Sometimes the crowds were so thick around the bandstand that Burgess had hardly room to move his arms. Squabbles arose; the police were called to regulate the traffic.

Another hazard was the weather. But the band played on, whether there were ten people or a thousand listening. And the band was always there, on the dot. Burgess was a stickler for punctuality. His band started to play even if a player was missing: 'It was our rule that a late-comer was not allowed on the bandstand until the finish of the piece we were playing and then when he did come aboard all the other players stood and played a chord to welcome him. I was caught only on two occasions myself – but I got the full treatment and didn't the young devils enjoy themselves!' Sometimes the rain drove straight into the bandstand, and the orchestra, with its instruments and music, re-formed inside a shelter, but the programme was finished: 'There were no programmes cancelled because of rain,' says the ex-bandmaster of the 2/5 Durham Light Infantry. In those early years, printed programmes did not exist. Each day Burgess wrote out the pieces to be played and pinned the paper on a little wooden notice-board by the bandstand. Devotees, pencil in hand, queued to copy the programme.

Burgess's first season was extended to mid-October: 'We were playing well but still I was not satisfied with many things.' He had a regular 9 a.m. Friday rehearsal – in a builder's yard,

whither an attendant pushed a handcart containing the drums
and the music stands. October came, the orchestra dispersed
to the cinemas and the theatres; Burgess himself wintered as a
violinist with the Scottish Choral Union, now the Scottish
National Orchestra, with the Carl Rosa Opera Company, the
D'Oyly Carte Opera Company, or with ships' orchestras playing
between Liverpool and the United States.

But as Easter drew near, Burgess homed on Weston like a
musical pigeon. He branched out. He engaged vocalists. With
twelve players he tried out the classical symphonies. However,
the time – at Weston, at any rate – was not ripe. During 1922
and 1923, he writes, 'Saxophones were beginning to groan their
way into the public notice, as also was the music with which they
were usually associated. I, imagining myself to be a "serious"
musician, detested these dance tunes and would not play them
but, like poor Canute, couldn't stop the rolling tide, and found
myself being drowned with such a number of "requests" that
I had to succumb! So I had to induce our clarinet and flute
players to buy an instrument and learn to play the saxophone
during the winter months to be ready to play dance tunes
during the next season.' His 'cellist took up the banjo; other
musicians became 'double-handed', earning an extra 5s a week
in order to play the phenomenally popular 'Dardanella', and
the various 'Top Ten' of the day. Ketelbey came on the scene.
'Will you ask the orchestra to play "In a Monastery Garden"?'
was often requested of a chair attendant. Waggishly, he replied
'Why? They're not THAT bad!' When asked 'Will they play
"In a Persian Market"?', his response was: 'Yes, but who's
going to pay the fare?' Sometimes the penny did not drop,
with adverse effects for the chair attendant.

Burgess loved Weston, Weston – and its Welsh patrons –
loved Burgess; and the collecting boxes chinked richly. This
did not prevent the Corporation (the band was now municipal)

from proposing its substitution by military bands, until 'it was ascertained that the cost of each band was about three times the cost of the orchestra'. If not, then at least Burgess's men should don bright uniforms. Burgess did not agree. 'We are British Musicians, not concert party performers, or yet pink or blue Hungarians and I would have none of it.' However he acquiesced in a uniformity of dress; the band appeared in navy blue, serge suits. Another season they wore black coats and striped trousers – they looked like undertakers, Mrs Burgess complained, so later all wore light grey suits; it was the summer, it was the seaside. And for all this uniform changing who was to pay? Burgess arranged with Messrs Burtons, the Tailors of Taste, to provide the light grey suits; in return each of his players would pay Burgess 5s a week hire-purchase until the instalments were cleared. A dozen suits at three guineas each and twenty-five shirts at 7s 6d were provided.

In 1927, with great pride, the Corporation opened its expensively-built Winter Gardens Pavilion and asked Burgess and his band to stay on through the Autumn to provide a morning string quartet, salon concerts and, twice a week, dance music. They wanted a quick return on the money. Burgess agreed and then discovered that, expensively-built or not, no one had thought about acoustics: the Pavilion was as full of echoes as a gorge in the Atlas Mountains, though not so beautiful. Burgess also agreed to a winter salary cut from £15 to £12 a week and for his band one of 5s. 'I can't blame my employers, because I hadn't the guts to fight,' he says.

In everything else he was dauntless and enterprising. Although potential winter audiences came only from Weston itself – population then under ten thousand – he lured them with such extraordinary performances as 'H.M.S. Weston-super-Mare' in which the orchestra dressed itself up and scenery and props were provided to resemble the deck of a warship. Burgess himself dressed as a naval officer and sea songs and shanties, hornpipes and special sketches were offered to the public at 1*s* a person. In return he persuaded his employers to allow him to present celebrity concerts in 1937–8, subscribers paying £1 each for four concerts. Some 364 subscribed. Patrons were asked to come in evening dress and, says Burgess, 'I confess the sight of that glamorous audience waiting to welcome us at the first of these concerts made me a proud and happy man.' Pouishnoff, Elisabeth Schumann and Moiseiwitsch performed with his eighteen-man orchestra.

Every week there was a classical concert. This was oddly arranged. Burgess would play two movements of a symphony, which was followed by a performance by a distinguished outside soloist. After the interval came the symphony's last two movements – then 'Ragamuffin Whistler' by Prior and 'Two Guitars' by Ferraris. Once he ventured to play Tchaikovsky's Fifth Symphony (omitting the third movement), observing in the programme note: 'In deference to the wishes of a few patrons, I am submitting this symphony without interruption, but I invite further expressions of opinion, particularly from listeners who have not long experience of listening to symphonies. Do you find the concentration for such a period too long? Or do you agree that it is a mistake to spoil the continuity of the work by interpolating a soloist? I should like opinions.'

Did he get them? I do not know; but he went on playing a symphony in two parts, one before and one after the interval.

Exactly how, with eighteen players or less, did he perform such massively orchestrated works as *Till Eulenspiegel*? One edition, approved by Richard Strauss, cued in all the parts and the 'bones' of the structure were clearly indicated. No less than three rehearsals were called by Burgess before he presented this work. The horn solo was played by the piano in octaves and subsequent woodwind motives were covered in the same way. The bassoon notes were cued in for trombone and 'cello; or for piano if there were no trombone or 'cello. The trumpets had the most important horn notes and these took precedence except when the brass demands in the score were paramount.

Burgess prides himself on the fact that all his programmes were freshly compiled – not repeated each month like a boarding-house menu. But he also knew that whatever success he had, without rehearsal, was due to his players: wonderful, tantalising, eccentric and occasionally rebellious men starting life with high ambition – some of them achieving it in London later, others perhaps growing cynical, alcoholic, *blasé* as the seasons ticked by.

One who did neither was Sie Foxhall, an ex-miner from South Wales who played three seasons at Weston in the 1920s. 'In subsequent years,' Burgess says, 'I heard many trumpet players in various parts of the country, but never did I hear a player with such a delightful tone and such exquisite artistry. His playing was a joy to listen to, the envy of his colleagues – including the conductor. . . . Alas, I couldn't afford to keep him and he returned to work underground using his music as a part-time extra to augment his wages. I don't know what happened to him, but I hope the world proved kind to a delightful artist.'

What *did* happen to Sie Foxhall?

A very young Scottish horn player named Bull with little professional experience had been strongly recommended by his teacher, at that time the principal horn of the Scottish Orchestra. He proved a good player, but as he was unfamiliar with much of the repertoire he had to play everything at sight. Although to an experienced professional this did not present great difficulties, it was not easy for him. Burgess told me how:

There came a time when we had on the programme the music from the ballet *Sylvia* by Delibes in which occurs an important solo for the horn. As his reading was not too good, Bull missed his entry. The trumpet player, quick to notice the omission, immediately started to play the solo which was cued in his copy. While this was taking place, an astonished orchestra saw the figure of Bull jump from his seat and, in a broad Scotch accent, yell across the bandstand to the trumpeter 'Hey! You! That's a horn solo' (or as he pronounced it, a 'hor-run' solo). The incident takes on a significance only if it is realised that one of the unforgivable sins is for a player to pinch another fellow's solo spot. But in this instance he had missed it and his colleague was only trying to save the situation. Poor Bull, how the 'boys' teased him. For weeks afterwards he could never escape the enquiry from one player to another, 'Hey! Is that a hor-run solo?' He was very Scotch; he confounded us all at the end of the season by making a present of a black dress bow tie to each of his colleagues, despite all their teasing.

George Locke, the drummer, was the safety valve of the orchestra:

Often when an irate conductor was becoming tiresome in his demands or expectations, it was George who would come out with some facetious remark or wise-crack that had us all laughing, and eased the tension. He was most helpful to me in the early days as he used to act as my librarian, collecting and distributing the various music parts. I don't remember him losing his temper. Still in my mind's eye his round, good-tempered face retains the sense of fun and humour.

In early summer 1938, Burgess was conducting in the bandstand when a letter from a newly-appointed Entertainments Manager was handed to him informing him that the engagement of artists and soloists was to be taken out of his hands. He was called to a Council meeting, where a newly-elected Councillor made a slashing attack on a concert he had given the week before. It was the climax of a series of pinpricks and underhand opposition to him, motivated partly by small-town Councillors' jealousy of a man more prominently and permanently in the public eye than themselves and their rationalisation of it in criticism of the 'unpopular' nature of the programmes.

Harassed by preparing and conducting eighteen programmes a week, arranging artists for the winter season, typing all letters himself (on a typewriter bought by himself), Burgess resigned. 'I was tired, perhaps fed up. Looking back, I think I was foolish as I simply embarrassed loyal supporters of the orchestra both in and out of the Council and rejoiced the anti-orchestra faction. The resignation, when accepted by the Council, aroused a storm of protest from the public and meetings were arranged, Councillors petitioned, and much correspondence took place in both the *Gazette* and the *Mercury*.'

In fact the press – there was then more than one local paper – fired fierce raking shots into the Council. The *Weston Mercury and Somersetshire Herald* of 6 August 1938 spoke of the 'top of the local volcano crater' blowing off when it became known that the Borough Council had recommended the acceptance of Burgess's resignation, only however by one vote, ironically enough that of the Mayor, Alderman Butt, himself a music lover and for long a supporter of Mogg's military band. The paper wrote:

> Let there be no mistake about it. If those who, by their votes, supported or condoned the plottings against Mr Burgess had to face the electors tomorrow they would be shot out of their seats like ninepins. And an otherwise perfectly good Mayor would go with them!

Oddly, everyone on the Council who voted against Burgess lost his or her seat in the election following. And, added the *Weston Mercury*, Bridlington – a much smaller place than

Weston – ran two first-class orchestras paying Herman
Darewski and his band £450 a week and between £350 and
£370 a week for another orchestra conducted by Lionel Johns.
Big sums were lost but 'Bridlington knows that the losses are in
reality a splendid investment'. Some congenital defect or
deformity, the paper claimed, prevented the Weston Council
realising this. Moreover a band minus the man who made it
could never be the same again. Besides if Burgess went, there
went with him his music library, 'fully scored parts for all the
instruments covering an immense repertoire'. Burgess had
spent hundreds of pounds building this library out of his own
salary, a point totally forgotten by the 'menagerie-majority of
the Entertainments Committee' which was castigated for
offering him revised terms of £575 a year – £11 a week.

That is their idea of a brilliant orchestral director and
musician; offering him a salary at which a Mackey-Mooning[1]
jazz band conductor would scoff. And out of that £575 he
would be expected to spend a substantial sum on instrumental scores. Music? They do not know even the ele-
mentary meaning of the word; yet to countless thousands
of Westonians and visitors it means very, very much. Just
because in one phrase H.C.B. spoke his mind (and the truth!)
he is to go; and all the brilliant service he has given to the
town, its people and its visitors, to be forgotten.

Strong words – and partially effective: Burgess departed,
but with a cheque for over £300, a finely-bound volume with
the names of all subscribers in copper plate and tributes and
articles in Gothic script. There was a farewell concert in the
Knightstone Pavilion on 4 October 1938. Burgess played a
programme to please himself: the Grand March from *Tannhäuser*, two Hungarian Rhapsodies by Liszt which he had
orchestrated, the first movement of Grieg's Piano Concerto,

[1] A reference perhaps to a popular dance band led by Percival Mackey.

and Bratza playing two movements from Mendelssohn's Violin Concerto. After the overture to *Tannhäuser* came the cheque.

The orchestra played on, if slightly *diminuendo*. Mozart Allan, referred to earlier, took over for a season, followed by the pianist of the orchestra, Lemuel Kinsey. It continued to play during the Second World War and, sometimes augmented, became the Weston United Orchestra. In 1945 there was a musical festival when Basil Cameron conducted a Beethoven night. But soon the Rozel bandstand was reduced to tiny proportions and the days when the resort had its own band were over. Burgess himself joined the B.B.C. Midland Orchestra as conductor and later arranger.

I asked Burgess why the resort orchestras disappeared. By this time he was over eighty, and time had healed his hurts. He replied:

Broadcasting did it. Once music was a treat, an unusual sound, and people gravitated to the bandstands in the parks and promenades. Later with loudspeakers assailing them on every side at home and in public, they wanted to get *away* from music. The standard of broadcast playing set up a new standard for audiences. This new standard was not always achieved by the poorer type of orchestra and the man in the street was quick to display his newly-found critical faculty to condemn much that he heard.

Two Prima-donnas

7. Pause for Song:
Arias and Ballads

Miss Blare's been howling Wagner all night long;
Sweet Thames roar loudly, till she end her song.
               John Press, *On a Massive Soprano*

THE Victorians sang, how they sang and when they were
not singing they were whistling in the street! They sang
in the drawing room, the parlour and the nursery; they roared
in the music-hall and joined the choruses at the pubs which
built adjoining concert rooms for this purpose. Round camp
fires, at Vauxhall, on bicycles and tricycles like Mr Polly they
sang their hearts out down country lanes; they sang to nerve
themselves for a cold bath, in barrack rooms to nerve themselves for battle; and every school began and ended the day
with a hymn – 'New every morning is the love', 'Now the day
is over' – and games in the playground went to some such lilt
as 'In and out the window' or 'Fire on the mountain, run, run,
run'. They loved listening to singing, too: opera, operetta,
ballad recital, choir festival, Entertainment, Christy Minstrels,
Ethiopian Serenaders, and Revivalist Meetings (many of these

are attractively described in M. Willson Disher's *Victorian Song: from Dive to Drawing Room*).[1]

It was a love, almost an epidemic, the resort orchestras could not ignore. From the beginning the blare and crash of the overture and the swaying of the waltz were stilled for a vocal soloist – it also rested the overworked band – and in early days at the big resorts of Bournemouth, Harrogate, Buxton and Eastbourne for someone more surprising: the entertainer at the piano or the comedian pure and simple. Among such performers were T. C. Sterndale-Bennett and C. Thornley Dodge who at a Harrogate concert following the *Rienzi* overture sang at the piano Grossmith's 'Tommy's First Love' and his own 'An Old Gentleman's Story'. George Robey, celebrated on the music-hall, appeared at Buxton between Massenet's 'Scènes Pittoresques' and Elgar's 'Pomp and Circumstance March No. 1'. At Bournemouth between 1893 and 1924, Sir Dan Godfrey listed, as well as such dancers as Maud Allan and Pavlova, the 'entertainers (including reciters)' who had appeared in his programmes; among them were George Graves, George Grossmith with his gift for nonsense verses, Harry Tate in his red-nosed sketches, Sir Harry Lauder – who not only pretended to be mean but was, Dan Leno, Vesta Tilley and the incomparable, massive Corney Grain, seated sideways at the piano making the keys dance to his fairy-like touch, as he sang his own 'The Ole Black 'Oss':

> He was nearly thirty-three, and he'd one broken knee,
> And the other one warn't quite sound,
> And his two 'ind legs was more like wooden pegs,
> And he couldn't 'ardly put 'em to the ground . . .
>
> Drat that ole 'oss, I'm jolly glad he's gone!
> Oh! Ay! Oh! The stall in the stable's empty!
> Oh! Ay! Oh! And the ole black 'oss is gone!

[1] Phoenix, London, 1955.

The 'entertainers' gradually faded out of the resort orchestra programmes, though in the late 1930s the Margate Municipal Orchestra on Sunday evenings still put Layton and Johnstone, Julian Rose, the Hebrew comic, or Sandy Powell ('Can you hear me, mother?'[1]) between *Fra Diavolo* and German's Welsh Rhapsody. But there was no decline in the popularity of solo singers, only a retrenchment in the economic difficulties of the 1930s. In the first half a soloist almost always included an operatic aria – Verdi, Donizetti, Mozart, Rossini and Gounod were the favoured composers – and in the early days that great Victorian delight, Ambroise Thomas's setting (or adaptation of) *Wilhelm Meister* which he called *Mignon*, whose famous aria

> Knowest thou that fair land
> Wherein the citron grows

seemed to have a magical delicacy and enchantment. Other works much drawn upon were von Flotow's *Martha* which contained 'The Last Rose of Summer', Wallace's *Maritana* for 'Scenes that are brightest'[2] and 'Yes, let me like a soldier fall', and Michael Balfe's 'With other lips and other hearts' from *The Bohemian Girl*. In the second half the tendency was to the ballad – as indeed was the routine at Henry J. Wood's Promenade Concerts until the late 1930s.

The resort orchestras after all were in part heirs of the ballad concerts, the 'Grand Morning Concert' or 'Soirée Musicale' which for long delighted middle-class Londoners. The ballad concerts were a peculiarly Victorian institution, being given up and down the country and in London under the direction of

[1] Joseph Lewis, an early conductor of the B.B.C. Orchestra, had a cough code when he went on the air which informed his mother of his precise state of health.

> [2] Scenes that are brightest
> May charm awhile
> Hearts that are lightest
> And eyes that smile

– words by Edward Fitzball, based on the play, 'Don César de Bazan'.

such men as Sir Julius Benedict – the theatre conductor who composed the opera *The Lily of Killarney* – and under the financial aegis of publishers like Chappell at the Queen's Hall. These concerts at first comprised solo songs with a few piano or violin interludes. Later, because of flagging public interest, light orchestral music was introduced as well.

But what were these 'ballads'? The musicologist of the future might well be pardoned for scratching his head over the word, particularly as this musical type is already half forgotten. The ballads of the nineteenth and early twentieth centuries had little in common with those sung by the troubadours, 'Chevy Chase', 'The Outlandish Knight' or the 'Twa Corbies' – stark and simple dramatic narratives – nor with those written to comment on some specific event and passed round as printed broadsheets in the seventeenth and eighteenth centuries. Any connection with the ballads of Brahms, Liszt or Schubert is also hotly denied by the starchier musical academics. Rather they were the little songs, easy to play, easy to sing, and easy on the emotions, that attained enormous popularity in the Victorian drawing room, round the Broadwood upright. The essence of the Victorian ballad was to be lightly sentimental, lightly religious and lightly gay. Essentially they were nostalgic, not dramatic; they were intended to raise a slight sigh after the port and cigars, not a *crise des nerfs*; they were the antithesis of the brooding intelligence and psychological penetration of the songs of Hugo Wolf.

Ballads were not necessarily valueless musically, though many were. Certainly they were melodious, even though imitatively and in small compass; but the best of them rose to the level of Schubert's 'Who is Sylvia?', Schumann's 'Two Grenadiers' and Brahms's 'Wiegenlied'. Elgar wrote them and so did Vaughan Williams, perhaps for money since the 'royalty' ballad – publishers paid not only the composer but also the

24. *Frank Gomez broadcasting with his Whitby Spa Orchestra in the 1930s from the Floral Pavilion, often 'an over-heated greenhouse'*

25. *Professor James Wilson's Parade Orchestra at Bridlington in the 1860s: quadrilles and Beethoven*

26. *Alexander Glazounov: his last appearance in England was with the Eastbourne Municipal Orchestra*

27. *Dame Clara Butt: advised 'sing'em muck'*

28. *Guilhermina Suggia: a regular resort festival soloist, said to sniff while playing (from a portrait by Augustus John)*

singers to 'plug' ballads – could be greatly gainful; their publishers would engage famous singers at phenomenal fees to sing them, thus giving them wide advertising and so boosting sales of the sheet music. The fine tenor, Edward Lloyd, said in 1899 that 'The Holy City' was selling 50,000 copies a year, and that he was engaged to sing four times in a month at 250 guineas each time – on condition that he sang 'The Holy City' on each occasion.

It was not always the words of the ballad so much as the tune and general sentiment, and not so much the tune as the opportunity provided for a voice to trill and skip and reach a high note without falter or a deep note without losing pitch, which attracted resort audiences. They loved the coloratura of an operatic aria and gradually the ballad changed from a simple song suited to a drawing room amateur to something designed to display the trained power of a professional on the platform. Dame Nellie Melba is reputed – though she denied it – to have advised Dame Clara Butt before she started an Australian tour to 'sing 'em muck' – so long as the voice could be heard doing high dives and tight-rope acts. It never quite, or generally, sunk to that, but it cannot be denied that a certain amount of 'muck' was performed to the great satisfaction of the crowds.

Though his ballads seem not to have survived into the heyday of the resort bands, one of the earliest composers was the Leeds musician and lyric writer, George Linley, born in 1798, who was said by the 1860s to have written 'the words and music of more English ballads than any other composer'; among them were 'Little Nell', 'Ever of Thee' and 'Thou art gone from my gaze'. Others were Pinsuti, Mattei and Piccolomini, whose songs had faded by the 1890s. However, another most prolific ballad composer, Sir Frederic Cowen, could still hear his best-known songs at Eastbourne and elsewhere up to the 1920s. This did not entirely please him, partly perhaps because he was

a serious symphonic and opera composer, partly because, as
he says in his autobiography, *My Art and My Friends*, the most
celebrated of all his songs, 'The Better Land', had 'haunted
him' ever since he wrote it in the 1870s. What was even worse,
wrote Cowen, who did not lack a sense of humour, was that he
had parted with the copyright 'while the fiend was still in its
infancy', though he had received £300 for it – not bad, he
thought for an hour's work. The words incidentally were by
Felicia Hemans, the poet also responsible for *Casabianca* ('The
boy stood on the burning deck . . .').

Cowen, however, took his 'fiendish' success good-humouredly
enough to print in his autobiography a parody of 'The Better
Land' composed by George Grossmith and sung by him at a
private party:

> 'I hear thee speak of a Better Land,
> Written by young Freddy Cowen's hand.
> Mother, where did he get that tune?
> Where did he steal it? oh, tell me soon!
> Did it come from Handel's grand "Messiah"?
> Or Charlie Gounod's "Ave Maria"?'
>   'Not there, not there, my child!'
>
> 'Is it far away in some region old,
> A Corelli jig that Fred Cowen "bowled"?
> The copyright has long expired;
> He could crib two bars and still be admired;
> A cheque from Boosey would come in soon –
> Is it there, dear mother, he stole that tune?'
>   'Not there, not there, my child!'
>
> 'I know where it came from, my gentle boy.
> I know where he got it, that song of joy:
> Down at the "Star" in the city, my dear;
> But good little boys may not enter there –

The name of the song was "The Shoreditch Swell".
How he came to hear it I cannot tell,
But from that song in that Hall so grand
He certainly stole "The Better Land".
    It was there, it was there, my child!'

Cowen in his book goes far to defining this particular kind
of ballad – or rather one of his lyric writers, Robert Francillon,
does it for him in these verses:

When I survey the glorious scene
    A Ballad Concert shows –
The singers dressed in pink or green,
    The audience all in rows –
To write a song I burn to try,
    A song – oh, pride to tell!
For Boosey's customers to buy,
    And Boosey's self to sell.

    And now I've got to do the trick
        Without a fear at all,
    That Fred won't find a tune to tick-
        Le up the Albert Hall.

Yes, I have got to write a song;
    At least, I've promised to.
They tell me it must not be long,
    Or else it will not do.
In just two stanzas there must be
    A little story jammed,
Or else 'twill never sell, you see,
    And surely will be d——d.

    And oh, a short refrain must come
        With sentimental tears,
    For Fred to make a tune to hum,
        And tickle people's ears.

'Why?' has been asked to death, I find;
　　And emptied is the theme
Of babies troubled with the wind,
　　And things that were a dream.
The publishers their counters cram
　　With pigeons by the load;
If half a subject's left, I am –
　　To put it meekly – blowed.

　　　Yet oh, a subject very soon
　　　　Is wanted, woe is me!
　　　For Fred to tickle with a tune
　　　　The ears of 'General P.'
　　　(Who's 'General P.'? Why 'General P.'
　　　　Is 'General Public' – don't you see?)

Were I that mighty minstrel who
　　To bed did Lily pack,
Or told us Doves are fair – as though
　　A jackass thought them black –
Then were I not in this sad fix,
　　And light would be the toil
To please the man that finds the sticks
　　That make the pot to boil.

　　　And Boosey is his noble name,
　　　　And gladly would I know
　　　The way to get but half the fame
　　　　Of those 'Long 'Ears ago.'

Yet if I mind the grand receipt
　　For making ballads do –
The little story, and the neat
　　Refrain, in stanzas two –
Perhaps I can't go very wrong,
　　Although of thoughts I'm bare,
If Nilsson will but sing the song,
　　And Cowen write the air.

> Oh, popular would even be
> In hands like theirs, I vow,
> The words of that wild melody
> That killed an aged cow.

But this is too strict a definition to contain all the songs or even ballads sung at the resort concerts. Most of the royalty ballads were poor musically and verbally, though some great singers made the poorest sound like fine music; but some were not. John L. Hatton's 'To Anthea' and 'Simon the Cellarer', both immensely popular with resort audiences, are excellent ballads, though others he composed are justly forgotten. Equally popular at the resorts were Loewe's fine 'Edward' and his 'Erl-King' and the traditional 'Shepherd, see thy horse's foaming mane', or Mussorgsky's 'Song of the Flea'. Sullivan's 'The Lost Chord' has no doubt become risible – it was so popular as to be a music-hall joke – and there is perhaps no more to be found now than a period atmosphere in James L. Molloy's 'Love's Old Sweet Song', May Brahe's 'Bless This House' and 'The Old Stone-house', and Ethelbert Nevin's 'The Rosary'. But Eva del'Acqua's 'Villanelle', Easthope Martin's 'Come to the Fair' or Landon Ronald's phenomenally successful 'O Lovely Night' do not in their differing ways lack charm. And what of Sir Francesco Paolo Tosti's 'Goodbye' sung in English to the words of Whyte-Melville?

> The swallows are making them ready to fly,
> Wheeling out on a windy sky,
> Goodbye, summer, goodbye, goodbye!
> Goodbye to hope, goodbye, goodbye!

There is too the everlasting Stanford setting of Graves's 'Father O'Flynn' –

> Powerfullest creature and tenderest teacher,
> And kindliest creature in old Donegal.

– which like J. P. Knight's 'Rocked in the cradle of the deep', prime favourites at the resorts which, I should be sad never to hear again.

Edward Purcell's 'Passing By' or Teresa del Riego's 'Homing'[1] are perhaps beyond the pale, and so for other reasons is Sir Henry Bishop's 'Home Sweet Home' – written incidentally as part of his opera *Clari* produced in 1823. But his 'Lo, hear the Gentle Lark' (with flute obbligato) remains pleasing; so does Graham Peel's often-sung setting of Housman's 'In Summer-time on Bredon' and 'Ettrick'.

'Bush Silence' and 'The Stock Rider's Song' by the Australian William James, who was also a concert pianist and composer, were often sung at the resorts; so were Marjorie Kennedy-Fraser's 'Eriskay Love Lilt', John Ireland's setting of Masefield's 'Sea Fever', Coleridge-Taylor's 'Eleanore', Frank Bridge's 'O That it Were So', and Vaughan Williams's 'Linden Lea', 'Bright is the Ring of Words' and 'The Vaga-bond'. Good or bad? The audiences certainly liked them as they liked Wilfred Sanderson's songs, Frederick Clay's 'I'll Sing Thee Songs of Araby' and 'The Sands of Dee', Stephen Adams's 'The Holy City', Carrie Jacobs-Bond's 'Just a Wearyin' for You' and Tierney's 'Little Alice Blue Gown'. Somewhat later, almost at the end of the period, came the ballads of Alan Murray – 'I'll Walk Beside You', 'Nut Brown Ale' and 'There is a Ladye'. Murray was a former director of the Royal Academy of Music.

No doubt the resort audiences were as undiscriminating over songs as they were discriminating over voices. They liked Stanford's 'Songs of the Sea', and Tate's 'For Love's Dear Sake' and Molloy's 'Kerry Dance' and Aitken's 'Sigh no More, Ladies'. They liked the ballads of Guy d'Hardelot and Maude Valerie White. In Sir Malcolm Sargent's time as conductor at

---

[1] Miss del Riego died in 1968, aged 91.

Llandudno in 1926–7, they listened rapt to 'Siegfried's Journey
to the Rhine', followed by Leveridge's ballad 'Advice' followed
by Schubert's 'Unfinished' Symphony. It was most repre-
hensible, though in matters less dominated by the *snobisme*
bred of academies, their taste might have been called catholic.

As the century drew on, in came good songs by such gifted
composers as Montague Phillips – 'The Fishermen of England'
and 'Waiting for You' – Roger Quilter ('Go Lovely Rose'),
Herman Lohr ('Little Grey Home in the West' and 'Where my
Caravan has Rested'), Sheridan Gordon ('Love, Could I Only
Tell Thee') and Haydn Wood. It is said that Wood made
£100,000 from a ballad written in 1916 called 'Roses of
Picardy'; its subject was, obliquely, English soldiers at that
time being slaughtered north-west of Paris; then and for long
after it left few audiences dry-eyed. Was that bad? Even today
'Roses of Picardy' recalls the anguish of mothers, fathers,
sisters and sweethearts at that ghastly destruction of the young
loved in a way that nothing else can. Bliss's *Morning Heroes* is a
fine and moving work – which receives three performances in
forty years; 'Roses of Picardy' has received three thousand in
the same period. Wood, in fact, is an underestimated composer;
not only do his highly popular ballads – 'Birds of Love Divine',
'Brown Bird Singing' – retain their cool poignancy, but his
violin concerto, his Manx rhapsody and his 'The Little Ships'
cantata about Dunkirk are not unworthy of revival.

Another composer of ballads of a more delicate air was
Michael Head, who set poems of Christina Rossetti, W. H.
Davies, Housman ('Ludlow Town'), Hardy ('Foxgloves'), Edith
Sitwell and John Drinkwater; 'I Arise from Dreams of Thee'
and 'You Shall Not Go A-maying' were accepted with satisfac-
tion at the resorts. So was Sir Walford Davies's 'When Childher
Plays' (words by T. E. Brown) and Peter Warlock's 'In an Ar-
bour Green' or 'How Many Miles to Babylon ?'. Rutland Bough-

ton's 'Faery Song' from his *The Immortal Hour* was sung alongside the more romantic ballads – for that is what they were – from, for instance, Léhar's operettas and the musical comedies of Romberg, Léo Fall, Victor Herbert, Rodgers and Hart, Vivian Ellis, Noel Coward and Ivor Novello. Throughout the period many resorts ended their Sunday evening performance with the audience taking part in Liddle's 'Abide With Me'.

It is natural to consider the songs and ballads as being primarily the products of composers. But at one stage the writers of the lyrics had a commanding, even a superior, status. Eric Coates in his autobiographical *Suite in Four Movements* tells of his trepidation in approaching the highly successful lyric writer – Coates calls him poet – Fred E. Weatherly in the hope that he might deign to give him one of his lyrics to set. Weatherly did, and it became the best-selling 'Stonecracker John'. For the tyro ballad composer this was a great triumph. Weatherly incidentally wrote the words to 'Roses of Picardy', to 'The Holy City' and to 'The Boys of the Old Brigade'.

Those – and a myriad more – were the songs, but who were the singers? Many were already famous; some were 'resting' from opera or operetta; others were so celebrated that vast sums were paid them to have concerts at the resorts billed round them – Dame Clara Butt or John McCormack for instance. Others still were on their way up and the resorts were useful stepping stones; yet others had got as high as they were ever going to. The names were legion – Dora Labbette, Miriam Licette, Lilian Stiles-Allen, Elsie Suddaby, Tetrazzini, Astra Desmond, Mary Jarred, Megan Foster, Isobel Baillie . . . John Coates, Ben Davies, Hubert Eisdell, Melchior, Peter Dawson, Norman Allin, Heddle Nash, Robert Easton, Henry Wendon, Francis Russell. In fact it is safe to say that scarcely any singer in the top class did not once appear at the resort concerts.

Their hey-day was in the first three decades of the century.

In the years before the Second World War singers began to disappear from the programmes, mainly because after the financial crisis of 1930–1 resorts were forced to economise on concert expenditure and visiting singers provided an obvious and individually fairly painless way of doing so. The better resorts concentrated more on solos by the highly talented instrumentalists in their orchestras though these, too, began to thin out when the B.B.C. formed permanent orchestras with annual salaries and pensions. When the singers left, some of the magic went too. The exquisitely gowned and coiffured lady – embarrassing with physical riches though she sometimes was, and 'difficult' as she might be behind the scenes – or the handsome baritone sleek in his tails, frilled shirt and buttonhole gave a sense of occasion to the evening concerts on the Spa or in the pier pavilion. Without them, platforms banked with roses, azaleas or hothouse chrysanthemums seemed sometimes to be waiting for the Prince and Princess who never came.

8. Great and Small:
Bantock to Darewski

Lynch the conductor! Jugulate the drums!
Butcher the brass! Ensanguinate the strings!
Throttle the flutes!...
     Siegfried Sassoon, *Stravinsky's April Comes*

A good question in a history of English music examination
might be: Who was the musician, later knighted, who for
three years conducted a dance band and with that band also
played Wagner, Elgar, Holbrooke and Berlioz? One clue is that
the concerts took place at a seaside resort not very many miles
from Liverpool and another is that the conductor concerned
has gone down into history as a composer.

The answer is: Sir Granville Bantock, later Professor of
Music at Birmingham University. The place: New Brighton at
the mouth of the Mersey. The time: 1897–1900. It is a curious
story. New Brighton, on a beach in the Wirral where Perch
Rock lighthouse signalled the ships into Liverpool, was up and
coming as the great port's Coney Island (they were connected

by ferry) and in 1895 it decided to build a tower like those of Paris and Blackpool. The Council advertised for a manager, and the young composer Bantock, out of work and in despair, applied. He pinned his faint hopes to some experience in the theatrical world. Son of a celebrated surgeon, he had graduated from the Royal Academy of Music in 1893 and – though he knew composing was his life – he had toured the provinces conducting for a burlesque, *Little Boy Blue*, and later as conductor of George Edwardes's touring Gaiety companies, performing *The Gaiety Girl, Gentleman Joe* and *In Town*. He had done Stanford's *Shamus O'Brien*, and *L'Enfant Prodigue* by André Wormser at the Royalty Theatre, London. After that nothing. He could not even obtain a tutoring post at the Royal Academy of Music or the Guildhall School of Music.

He was no luckier with his application to be Tower manager at New Brighton; he did not even get an acknowledgment. He forgot about it. Then six months later he received a letter saying that, though the post of manager had been filled, New Brighton Tower required a musical director. He accepted gladly. When he arrived the tower, 612 feet tall, was barely completed. In the circular red brick building at its base was an enormous ballroom and there Bantock was to play for dancers in the evening. During the day he was to conduct a military band – in the open air surrounded by a fairground, a menagerie, tight-rope exhibitions by Blondin and, not far off, merry-go-rounds, shooting galleries and steam organs. Horses galloped across the beach to the screams of their holiday-making riders, boats whistled, waves pounded: Coney Island indeed.

Bantock was to conduct his band – the personnel were identical whether playing military or dance music – for five or six hours a day including Sundays. Waltzes, barn dances and polkas were the evening fare; Sousa, Suppé, 'Samson and

Delilah' the morning. He fulfilled his duties punctiliously. The money began to roll in and the management were pleased. Thus encouraged Bantock suggested that the ballroom band might also be used to give concerts. Approval was given and, still conducting the dance band every evening from 7.30 to 10.00, he began light orchestral programmes on weekday afternoons. At first he was cautious. One extant programme is far from revolutionary. He began with the Coronation March from 'Henry VIII' by German, 'Moonlight on the Rhine' waltz by Vollstedt, polka 'Chu Chin Chinaman' by Kierfert, Wald-teufel's waltz 'Très Joli', selection from Sidney Jones's 'The Geisha', Strauss's 'Blue Danube', 'Invitation to the Polka' by Thomé and the galop 'Troika Race' by Damaré.

Then, bang, on a Friday afternoon in June 1898, Beethoven's 'Egmont' Overture, Mozart's 'Jupiter' Symphony, the Siegfried Idyll and Liszt's Second Hungarian Rhapsody. Subsequent Fridays had Dvorak's 'From the New World' Symphony, Tchaikovsky's 'Pathétique' Symphony, Rubinstein's 'Ocean' Symphony, all the Beethoven Symphonies, and grand all-Wagner concerts.

Such sounds had never before been heard in the Cheshire Coney Island and probably were never heard again. Nor did it end there. Emboldened by success or at any rate lack of criticism – perhaps the committee had not heard? – Bantock began a Sunday series of concerts with a 100-strong orchestra of the works of living composers, largely English, and where possible conducted by themselves. Cowen, Parry, Elgar, Corder and Wallace all visited New Brighton to conduct their own compositions. Mackenzie came, and new works were given by Hinton, Hamish McCunn, Holbrooke, Bell and many others. For eighteen Sunday concerts the subscription was 10s 6d.

It was *épatant*! To hear Elgar, much less Holbrooke, at New

Brighton in 1899 was as improbable as to hear Stockhausen or Boulez in Margate's Dreamland today. The programmes became famous, at least among musicians. *The Musical Times* wrote of 'a splendid series of concerts' and mentioned performances of Bantock's own works including the 'Eugene Aram' overture, the Songs of Persia and the 'Dante' symphonic poem. Joseph Holbrooke's tone poem 'The Skeleton in Armour' was also picked out for mention. It was the fame of these performances that encouraged the young Dan Godfrey to feature new English works at Bournemouth.

Bantock's New Brighton concerts were a phenomenon, but so was Bantock. Later regarded as one of the most important English composers of the earlier part of the twentieth century, his compositions were vast in number, as in scope, and he was deeply interested in ideas and philosophies, particularly of the East, absorbing them as a dog absorbs bones. Something of an eccentric, at one time preferring to wear a velveteen suit rather than more normal dress, he was as prolific in his life as in his music, filling his house not only with his four children but also with animals, whom he loved to see eating; one of his great pleasures was to feed his fowls, pigeons, geese, dogs and tortoises. In his conservatory stood an enormous tank of goldfish. He bought books recklessly and then had to clear them out of his house for want of room. If he went to a new place he bought immediately at least fifty picture postcards of it. He was generous, open-handed and affectionate, much loved by his intimates and a great conversationalist, as Dan Godfrey records in *Memories and Music*. Godfrey also records his habit of offering his guests Canadian rye whiskey, jam and cheese which seemed to Godfrey 'the hallmark of eccentric refreshment'. He had a partiality for plums which he offered to friends and acquaintances on 'somewhat impossible occasions', such as the Gloucester Festival when in the Cathedral he suddenly offered one to a learned dignitary of the Church. He could not pass a sweet shop without buying; and like a number of professional musicians, he was a great leg puller.

By all accounts he was a very successful conductor, being resourceful, full of rhythmical vitality, with the power to bring out clearly all the points in the work being performed. Perhaps because he was basically a composer he was most averse to conductors who set themselves to produce new effects regardless of the original intentions of the composer. Nor did he go in for the slavish rehearsals of Wood or Godfrey. He was impatient of the finicking, meticulous anxiety of some conductors, preferring a more robust and simple style. Too many rehearsals, he believed, took vitality out of the final performance; the test of a great conductor, he thought, was not so much what he could do with a symphonic poem after weeks of laborious rehearsals as what he would do if in an emergency he was set to conduct an unknown work at a day's notice.

Practical though he was, his concerts of new English music at New Brighton could not and did not last. By 1900, the Directors became more and more hostile to him: the enterprise was not paying. Luckily Bantock was offered the post of Principal at the Midland Institute School of Birmingham. He took final leave of New Brighton in 1901 when he received from his orchestra an address regretting his loss and acknowledging the fine work he had done. Inevitably the band relapsed after his departure to their original status as an amusements band. And that was the end of the brief musical glory of New Brighton – or nearly the end, for there is a brief coda.

A few years later a small group under John Blamphin was playing light music in the Kursaal on the Pier at New Brighton. Occasionally the audiences were astonished to hear a movement from a Reinecke trio or something else of a kind totally out of the atmosphere of New Brighton. The reason for this was that three of the Goossens brothers, Eugene, Léon and Adolphe, then very young, all played in the Pier Band.

Few of the resort orchestra conductors reached the academic musical eminence of Bantock: an exception was Frederick Corder who had taught Bantock at the Royal Academy of Music as he also taught Bax, Holbrooke and others. Corder, after a late start at the Academy, and staying for only a year and a half, was elected to the Mendelssohn scholarship and sent to Cologne where he studied for four years under Ferdinand Hiller. Shortly after his return he was appointed conductor at the Brighton Aquarium, where, it is said, he raised the musical entertainments from the very low level at which he found them and brought the orchestra to a better condition of efficiency. For a time he also conducted in the theatre at Devonshire Park in Eastbourne. He was a composer whose works were performed at various festivals, he was the translator of *The Ring* and other works by Wagner and he conducted provincial tours of his own romantic opera *Nordisa*. From 1888 he was Professor of Composition at the Royal Academy of Music of which he became curator in 1889. His influence upon the course of English music was considerable – but of his programmes at the Brighton Aquarium no record now remains.

If Bantock and Corder represent the – zenith of resort music though their achievements in no way come up to the sustained work of such men as Godfrey at Bournemouth and Maclean at Scarborough – then Herman Darewski represents the nadir. Darewski, who performed at Blackpool (mainly as a dance band leader) and Bridlington, was universally liked by colleagues in many fields, but he was a harbinger of the fate which overtook many of the resorts as the 1930s went on. One of a large musical family, he brings a breath of the music-hall stage, of the Charing Cross Road, and of the new dance-mad world into these pages. He was a music publisher, he wrote songs, he performed on the stages of super-cinemas, he played the piano and he led bands. He loved dance music and jazz and stunts of every kind. In his *Musical Memories* he is frank about it. Not only had he no strong desire to perform first-rate music, whether of a light or more serious nature, but he was positively opposed to doing so in the resort atmosphere. Perhaps he had smarted under councillor criticism; at any rate he firmly believed that: 'To attempt to educate the public at a seaside resort is the biggest mistake that a conductor can possibly make.' The audience had to be given music they would enjoy – if they were to be educated musically that would be when they returned to the towns and to their duties: 'Classical music can puzzle and irritate the mind when simple and more melodious tunes can harmonise and lull the senses, achieving a drugging and restful effect', he wrote. Whether 'drugging' is necessary in music even at the seaside is a debatable point; there cannot have been much 'lulling' about the concerts of new English composers given by Bantock at New Brighton or by Godfrey at Bournemouth. What Darewski assumed was that no happy mean existed, that there was no public at the English resorts to take pleasure in a Beethoven symphony sandwiched between a selection from *The Gondoliers* and a waltz by Waldteufel.

He was wrong at the time of which he wrote, namely the 1920s and 1930s. Even in Blackpool itself in 1937 Jan Hurst with the South Pier Orchestra in the Floral Hall was regularly putting on programmes of a surprisingly mixed nature – one before me is of French composers which as well as light works by Thomas, Gounod and Massenet, included a performance of César Franck's Symphonic Variations for Piano and Orchestra and Saint-Saëns' Septet for piano, trumpet and strings. The same was true in Bridlington itself at the rival hall on the Prince's Parade.

Darewski arrived at the new Spa at Bridlington in the early

29. 'Which dress tonight?' Clarice Dunington with her Ladies' Orchestra in the Floral Hall, St Anne's-on-Sea, in 1921

30. The Pavilion, Torquay, where Basil Cameron and Ernest W. Goss conducted the Municipal Orchestra from 1912 to 1952

31. *Eldridge Newman, sensitive conductor of the Folkestone Municipal Orchestra (1928–1940); his end was a mystery*

32. *Sir Granville Bantock: conducted dance music and symphonies with the New Brighton Tower Band, 1897–1901*

33. *Captain Henry G. Amers, ~~musical~~ ical director of the Eastbo~~urne~~ Musical Festival and condu~~ctor~~ of the Municipal Orchestra*

1920s. It comprised a bandstand with a glass-covered dome and rows of form seats. At the back was a small row of shops and a café. It seemed to him, he tells us, ripe for development. At once he intimated his desire to cover the iron pillars supporting the glass roof of the dome with large cut-out figures of soldiers with tall busbies and rifles at their side and girls in poke bonnets with spreading skirts. The authorities refused. Soon, however, they allowed him to introduce dancing at the Spa; immediately the receipts jumped, and special trains and buses were required to bring people in to the Darewski Dances. The result was that a new Royal Hall – costing £50,000 and seating 4,000 – was erected in 1926 'which I can truly say I not only inspired but officially opened'. Not long after it was destroyed by fire – and an even finer Royal Hall went up in its place. This, he believed, gave Bridlington the finest dance and concert hall on the coast and was second only to the Albert Hall in capacity. It had a dancing floor, balconies, palm lounges, cafés and a solarium. Still, it needed stunts to fill it and stunts, Darewski says, he provided 'both novel and humorous, and I have spent long hours thinking out ideas that will bring the people in'. One stunt was his request to his audiences to bring in a rose from each garden in the resort so that they could be presented in a united bouquet to the Queen of Carnival at her coronation. Almost before he could turn round, 2,500 roses lay on the Royal Hall floor. With the aid of volunteers all were arranged into one huge bouquet and wired together. Four men were needed to carry it for the presentation to the Carnival Queen.

In fairness to Bridlington, there was other and better music as well, indeed a century of it this year (1967). When the Princes Parade was opened in 1867, Professor James Wilson's orchestra – it seems to have had no more than eight players including a harpist – played on a small mound in the open air and substantial profits were made out of the 3*d* daily, 1*s* weekly and 7*s* season tickets. There were long discussions in the local papers about the kind of music required, one particularly hurtful suggestion being that the taste of visitors was of a higher order than that of residents. The *Free Press* in October, 1867 wrote: 'One does not always care to be reading Dante and Milton – "Pickwick" and "Sam Slick" alike contribute their quota to the enjoyment and happiness of society; equally so does the elegant waltz or spirited quadrille inspire pleasurable emotions, although perhaps different from those produced by the works of Beethoven and Mozart. That our visitors alone have patronised the higher class of music is a simple untruth. On every occasion the inhabitants have formed a large majority of the audience, and why their musical taste should be impugned we are at a loss to imagine.'

A bandstand, then a Floral Pavilion were built and the orchestra prospered under such conductors as Charles Harvey, Sigmund Winternitz, Joseph Sainton and Enrico Scoma, coming to be known as the Municipal Orchestra. That title was lost after 1922 but, never of great size, the orchestra attained a growing repute under such men as Garadini, Hurst, Barker and Johns. After the war it diminished into a salon orchestra, flourishing under Reginald King. Today it is an all-purposes band of sixteen players.

Midway between the brash entertainment band and the large municipal orchestras came the small, musically undemanding groups such as the Ladies' Orchestra at St Annes-on-Sea, a 'refined' resort eight miles south of brazen Blackpool. An all-ladies orchestra was itself a novelty and drew crowds to the Pier 'Floral Hall' with its dozens of hanging baskets and, for one season only, quantities of Red Admiral butterflies, a bright idea of the Pier manager.

Each evening – there was also a morning performance – from Easter until 30 September, audiences waited for 7.45 p.m., rapt with speculation upon which gown tall Clarice Dunington, the conductor, would wear when she glided to the rostrum. One gown still graceful in memory was a floor-length sleeveless Liberty dress of chiffon velvet in a dark peacock hue with long white panels front and back upon which Miss Dunington's father had painted orchids. Miss Dunington was a violinist, a member of the Hallé Orchestra as was her sister Maud, a 'cellist, and like most members of the Ladies' Orchestra had studied at the Royal Manchester College of Music. On special guest nights Miss Dunington's husband, the celebrated bassoonist Archie Camden – they had met while in the Llandudno Pier Orchestra – would appear to render such bassoon classics as 'Lucy Long'. The Ladies enjoyed St Annes, being constantly invited out to 'high' tea (invariably fresh salmon and salad, fruit salad and cream and rich home-made cakes). They swam and acquired a fine sun-tan very becoming against their white evening gowns; they golfed; and some rode horses along the cart tracks over the Fylde.

The Ladies dispersed around 1932 and were replaced by a mixed band and during the war the orchestra was reformed under F. Lionel Johns, formerly at Bridlington. He had been a Hallé violin player who early in the dance-mad 1920s launched out as Don El Varro, master of a tango band. Johns, tall, dark and handsome, quickly became the 'idol of St Annes'. Among his innovations was the painting of his music stands and piano white. He allowed no break between the items so that the audience would not start chattering. On Tuesday mornings he had forty or fifty children on the platform, some of whom he allowed to conduct. There were guest nights and nights when the audience themselves entertained. Johns himself would sing an occasional ditty. The Floral Hall was bright and cosy. Tea was served and since St Annes was on the West coast away from the danger area of bombs, it flourished greatly and still continues to do so, although Johns retired in 1966 aged 73 and his place has now been taken by Norman George, a former player with the B.B.C. Northern Orchestra.

There was here in Johns's time no pretence either at educating the audience or playing anything more demanding from the classical repertoire than a Mozart Overture or a Beethoven Minuet. The staple fare was selections from musical comedies new and old, Ivor Novello, Rudolph Friml and Sigmund Romberg, *Oklahoma*, *My Fair Lady*, and *The Sound of Music*. All was bright and tuneful as the teacups clattered. The musicians had to be able and, of course, willing to perform under such arch descriptions as 'Myra and her mellow 'cello' or 'Triplets – Beatrice, Gillian and Doreen'. The pianist for many years was Doreen Fennell who from time to time appeared as Doreen Flannel, 'Be prepared – ready for anything', in something approaching a music-hall sketch. It was mild, vaguely amusing and most certainly 'lulling'. As Johns himself noted: 'I play for the middle-aged couples. They send their children off to a dance in Blackpool, and then listen to me and the old favourites.'

9. Eastbourne:
The Duke and the Municipality

Ah, not again to quicken
The grieving willows of the strings,
The autumnal oboe,
The desolate bright trumpet,
To summon lost imaginings
From Edens stricken.
            Stanley Snaith from *The Common Festival* (1950)

MUSICALLY speaking, Eastbourne was different from all the other English resorts. A mere village in the 'rape' of Pevensey 150 years ago, it grew quickly into a solid, even stylish, home-from-home for well-to-do Victorians. It was never a spa though, desiring to be in the spring as well as in the swim, early guide books refer tentatively to its chalybeate Holywell, and from the 1890s vans carried hot or cold sea-water to any part of the town at any hour, price 3*d* a bucket hot and 2*d* a bucket cold – an enlightening commentary both on hotel bathrooms and attitudes to sea-bathing.

This comfortable town at first followed the usual musical

pattern of 'Herrs' – Herr Wolf, Herr Mann and Herr Fritz successively conducting the town band from about 1850, and then came the Blue Hungarians under – possibly for once a genuine Hungarian gipsy – Darazs Yozsef who had performed before the Prince of Wales at Marlborough House, and James Hamilton with his Orchestre Militaire who, as far as I know, never performed anywhere except at Eastbourne in the 1890s.

But the pattern was decisively broken in 1874 – broken to give Eastbourne a permanent orchestra of near-symphonic size earlier than any other resort. This body of players was called the Devonshire Park Orchestra, though it had mutations into the Duke of Devonshire's Private Orchestra, later the Duke of Devonshire's Eastbourne Orchestra. It came about in this way: much of the land upon which the town of Eastbourne was built belonged to the Devonshire family, Compton Place being the seat of Lord George Cavendish at the beginning of the nineteenth century. In 1874 the then Duke, with an eye to future profit in the developing resort, opened a park with a theatre, concert hall, baths, a skating rink and other amenities. An orchestra was formed, its earliest conductor being the Julian Adams we have met twice before in these pages. On his death in 1887, a London musician, Norfolk Megone, then twenty-seven, was appointed. After studies in Germany he had founded the Belsize Amateur Orchestral Society and in 1882 the Strolling Players Amateur Orchestral Society (which he conducted until 1902). He composed waltzes including *Oenone*, and had a number of theatre appointments. A dark man with large, smiling face and small waxed moustache, he remained with the Devonshire Park Orchestra except for one or two years until 1917, though only for the summer season. In the winter when the orchestra, sometimes with different personnel, was known as the Duke of Devonshire's Eastbourne Orchestra, his place was taken by Pierre Tas. The town already regarded itself as a cut above its rivals – 'the demands of the visitor in Eastbourne are in advance of what is required at most watering-places', the guide observed in 1894 – and this is reflected in a note about Megone and his orchestra in the 1891 *Prospectus of Devonshire Park*:

> No effort will be spared by the gifted conductor (whose fame in the metropolis grows daily greater) to place before Subscribers and the public programmes of the highest excellence and of the most recherché character. In addition to the orchestral performances, arrangements have been made by which at least one vocalist will appear at every evening concert throughout the entire season, with special concerts on Saturday evenings, classical concerts on Thursday evenings and grand concerts with 'Eminent Stars' at longer intervals.

Among such stars in that same year of 1891 were mentioned Madame Dotti, Mr Maybuck, Mr Bantock Pierpont, Mr Plunkett Greene and Madame Annette Essupoff. Harry Plunkett Greene, an Irish bass-baritone singer, excelled in Brahms and Schumann songs, and appeared in opera and at the Gloucester Festivals. Many of Stanford's songs were written for him.

Just how 'recherché' Megone's concerts were is difficult to establish, since most of his programmes have disappeared. Certainly his objective was good for in a programme note in 1904 he observed that 'within the past few years a school of young composers of British parentage has arisen. At last a school of English music is in being whose productions in time bid fair to rank with the best of those of the Continental schools' – and presumably he presented some of these compositions. One of Tas's winter programmes of items selected by the vote of the public is, however, extant for Sunday, 16 February, possibly 1906 – unfortunately concert promoters too seldom print the year as well as the date. The Sullivan overture 'In Memoriam' shared first place with the overture to

Beethoven's *Fidelio*, then Gounod's famous 'Hymne à Sainte Cécile', played on this occasion by the violinist Sidney Freedman and Miss Cockerill, the harpist. Popular taste obviously favoured overtures, for those to Mackenzie's *The Cricket on the Hearth* and Wagner's *Rienzi* were also on this programme. Chamber concerts were also given by members of the orchestra; in this same month could be heard Berlioz's Trio for two flutes and harp and Richard Strauss's Serenade for Wind Instruments. The admission to this concert, which included other items, was 1*s* while subscribers entered free.

A symphony concert on 27 February, as well as Brahms's Symphony No. 1 and Mendelssohn's Piano Concerto in G Minor, contained two items seldom if ever heard in later days – the overture to *Shylock* by a young English composer called Felix, who was largely self-taught and became moderately well-known for his chamber music and for his translation of Hindemith's operas *Cardillac* and *Mathis der Maler*, and a suite 'Song of the Swiss Mountains' by Hathaway whom I have not been able to trace. Other symphonies now seldom played were those by Gade, Goldmark ('Rustic Wedding'), Raff and Sterndale Bennett.

Thursday nights were classical nights; there were occasional Wagner nights – even in 1894, and on Saturday monster concerts were given followed by fireworks. For example 'Mr Norfolk Megone's Grand Concert' was given on 5 September 1906 when along with his own Devonshire Park Grand Orchestra – of fifty-four players, including such later well-known names as John Bridge, Charles Draper the clarinettist and Victor Watson, double bass, and with four horns, five cornets and six trombones as well as a tuba and a euphonium – there was the band of His Majesty's Coldstream Guards, the band of the 2nd Sussex R.G.A. Volunteers, the pipers of the Scots Guards, and the municipal orchestra and military band. The concert

was referred to as being of 'great length' and it was therefore
earnestly requested that 'encores should in no case be insisted
on, as many visitors from the country have to catch the last
train'. It began with the Grand March from *Le Prophète* by
Meyerbeer, Wagner's *Rienzi* and Tchaikovsky's '1812' overtures along with songs by the operetta singer Evie Greene,
Nellie Dunford (pupil of Sir Charles Santley) and Charles
Copland. It was Miss Dunford's first appearance and she sang
Cowen's famous 'The Swallows' and Batten's 'The Nightingale'.
The ubiquitous Thornley Dodge, 'Humorist', sang his own
songs and others by Corney Grain and Grossmith ('Tommy's
First Love'). Curiously enough at this late date, the concert
ended with Jullien's 'The British Army Quadrilles'. It may be
of interest to give the synopsis as printed on the programme:

Encampment at night. Sentries passing the call, 'All's
well' – (*tempo di marcia*) – patrol going the rounds visiting
sentries – sentries again passing the call, 'All's well' – twilight
appears and the day breaks – the trumpet sounds Reveille
and the whole camp is soon in motion – the troops fall in and
the trumpet announces the DEPARTURE.

PARADE of the troops, quick march, performed by the
orchestra and the military band.

MUSIC OF THE INFANTRY regiments on parade, 'The
Dashing White Sergeant' with variations for the principal
soloists of the orchestra.

Introduction (*Allegro*) followed by combined flourish of
cornets – music descriptive of field exercises of the artillery.

Music of the Cavalry Regiments – galloping of the horses.

Introduction to No. 6 Night – 'Go to bed Tom' – all quiet
and regular – God Save the King (ppp) – (*Allegro*, troops of
the enemy heard advancing in the distance – foiled – they retire
– all quiet – God Save The King – (*Allegro*) enemy again
advancing – horses galloping – trumpets sound the challenge –
recit. by euphonium, descriptive of issuing the orders – the

alarm is sounded and repeated by distant buglers – (*agitato*) orders despatched for troops to assemble from their various encampments – first band heard approaching from the distance playing 'The British Grenadiers' March' – call for help – the second band is heard approaching playing 'Gerry Owen' – the troops call for further help – the Scotch pipers come to the support of their brothers in arms – trumpeters' call sounded, followed by that of the officers and Sergeant-Majors – they receive orders to form their troops up and to prepare for battle – finale – troops formed up for battle.

Troops marching on the enemy – battle music (*tempo di marcia*) – the attack on the enemy – fierce cannonade and musketry – battle rages – enemy retires completely routed – victory for the British Army – Hurrah! – GRAND FINALE: 'SEE THE CONQUERING HERO COME' and 'God Save The King'.

It must have been a stirring, exciting sound echoing through the Floral Hall and out across the moonlit park, with its multi-coloured foliage trees and shrubs, rockeries, yuccas, dracaenas and other sub-tropical vegetation (I quote the 1904 booklet). No less agreeable than the Floral Hall – warm and comfortable 'even when stormy winds howl' – was the 'closerie de peupliers' where on summer afternoons a band played while ladies in flowery dresses and gentlemen in bright tweeds strolled and chatted and took strawberries and cream for tea. This was the high afternoon of Edwardianism and elegant Eastbourne its most refined playground.

Meantime the Corporation was not falling behind. In 1893 at the cost of £300 it built a bandstand on the Royal Parade and the first performance was given by the band of the Brighton Corporation – surely *lèse-majesté* for Eastbourne. Not to be outdone by private enterprise, in 1898 a municipal orchestra was formed, its 27 members engaged and paid by the Corporation, and this replaced the town band. Its conductor was Theo

Ward, who was paid £350 a year. He gave his first performance on July 1, 1898. Ward is forgotten now except by one or two older inhabitants of Eastbourne who recall that he was music mad and that his rooms had scores everywhere on chairs, tables, floor and bookcases so that there was hardly room to move.

The municipal orchestra flourished but by 1906 the Council began to complain of its cost and cut it down to sixteen players. Three instrumentalists, oboe, bassoon and viola, were dismissed. Worse was to come. It had been suggested that Theo Ward with his reduced forces should play at a skating carnival. Councillor Climpson, however, objected. For the skating, he said, a barrel-organ would do just as well.

Supporters of the orchestra were outraged by the slur. They rushed into irate print in the local papers. So, too, did a piano-tuner called G. F. Grant, an inveterate writer of newspaper letters in which he always adopted a deep Somerset accent faithfully if bizarrely transcribed into print. This time he went further. He circulated through the town a printed, bogus 'programme of grand concerts during the winter evenings to be given by the grand municipal one-man orchestra'. The concerts would take place on the front in winter evenings, so chairs, foot-warmers and rugs would be available for hire. Because the Western bandstand had been let to a nigger troupe, rehearsals would take place in the Floral Hall – at intervals during the skating carnival. Programmes would include Theo Ward in the Pan Pipe Concerto in D Minor by Riff Raff; the cultured musical members of the Council would sing a part song called 'Every Cloud has its Silver Lining'. A song based on the Lay of the Last Minstrel would be amended:

> I cannot play the old tune
> Without my comrades three,
> Oboe, bassoon and viola,
> So rudely torn from me;

> But I will do my humble best
> With cymbal, drum and bell
> To justify the one man band
> And save the rates as well.

Chorus: Oh where and oh where
> Are my fellow minstrels gone ?
> They're gone to swell the band
> On some other seaside strand,
> And it salves [sic] my heart
> When from them I had to part.

There was to be a grand concert overture with original effects by Herr Climpsowski – a musical variant on the name of the unfortunate Councillor. He would also give grand organ recitals on the municipal street organ. And so on. It was all great fun and entertained the town for some weeks.

Ward sought refuge at Buxton, his successor being Major Hiram Henton. He, too, had his troubles. In 1912 a storm was reported to have blown up in the Eastbourne Town Council because 'Mr Henton, the conductor of the municipal band, turns his back on his men and faces the audience'. A Councillor wanted to know why when Eastbourne spent £4000 a year on its music, it should allow 'trifling in that way'. The habit was not uncommon, as we have seen. Perhaps the storm was part of an anti-orchestra movement for in 1913 the municipal band was dis-banded.

Behind this disbandment, however, lay motives other than economic. The Corporation had always been jealous of the fame of the Devonshire Park Orchestra and desired to take it, and the park itself, into municipal custody. As early as 1897 negotiations had taken place between the Corporation and the directors of the Devonshire Park Company over the possible purchase by the Corporation of the Winter Gardens, the Pavilion, the grounds and the baths; the terms, however, were not acceptable to the Corporation. In 1912 a Bill was promoted by the Corporation for the purchase of the Devonshire Park, but a poll of the rate-payers resulted in a majority against it and the Bill was withdrawn. The same thing happened again with the same result in 1914. But some cooperation was achieved: it was agreed that £6,600 should be allowed for the maintenance of an improved orchestra and that the Devonshire Park Company were to provide it and a military band. The band would have twenty-five players in the summer and twenty-one in the winter; the orchestra at the Devonshire Park was to be twenty-five in the summer and thirty-one in the winter. By 1913 the cost was estimated at about £7,336 a year of which the Corporation was to pay £3,960. The arrangement seems to have been little affected by the war; Norfolk Megone continued as conductor until 1917 when he was succeeded by Captain William MacBean and then by C. Emlyn-Williams.

A complicated reorganisation took place in 1919 when the general arrangement under which the Corporation and the Company shared the cost of the orchestra and the band was terminated. The Corporation decided to engage its own military bands. This seems to have been the last straw for the Devonshire Park Orchestra which made its final bow in 1922. From this time forward there was an Eastbourne municipal orchestra and a military band, many of the military band personnel playing in the orchestra in the evening. (It was not until 1931 that the Corporation actually purchased the Winter Gardens of the Devonshire Park and not until after the Second World War in 1946 did it finally purchase the Devonshire Park grounds and the Company come to an end.)

The herald of the new régime was Henry G. Amers, mentioned briefly above. Both his father and grandfather were professional musicians in the North of England, and he started his musical life as a chorister in the Church of St George's, Newcastle-on-Tyne, where he studied under the organist James M. Preston, and later in Germany. As a youth he played a solo by command before the Princess of Wales and several times before King Edward VII. For a time he conducted on the Palace Pier, Brighton. In 1914 he joined the Northumberland Hussars and served almost four years in France, was wounded and became assistant Provost Marshall at Hazebrouck, later to be given the command of a German prisoner-of-war camp. He was invalided home in 1919, awarded the Territorial Decoration for officers and became a Captain of the Reserve. He returned to Brighton in 1920 and was appointed to Eastbourne in October of that year.

Amers blossomed forth in Eastbourne and there was formed a society of 'friends of the orchestra' which was really an Amers fan club. He was much admired by lady members of the audience; he seems to have been a kind and sympathetic music director. Always immaculately dressed, he wore a red carnation in his buttonhole and red hair to match. In the 1920s, Amers's hey-day, the town was placarded with notices announcing 'Grand Parade Bandstand. Every morning at 11, Captain H. G. Amers and his Famous Band'. At that time the Grand Parade bandstand was a cast-iron erection like a bird cage on stilts growing out of the shingle beach. The stilts brought it up to the level of the middle parade where the deck chairs (3*d* a session) were set out. The approach to the bandstand was by way of an iron staircase leading up from the lower parade where the seats were harder and cost only 2*d*. The band was smartly dressed in a blue and red uniform and Amers himself wore his uniform cap at a jaunty angle. Quite in the style of the old 'Herrs', Amers did not arrive for the morning, military band concert until the second item, the opening march generally being left to the deputy conductor who was one of the clarinettists. After a short pause as the deputy conductor threaded his way back to his seat, Captain Amers briskly ascended the stairs and took up his baton for the second item which would be either a popular overture or 'reminiscences' of one of the great composers. This was invariably followed by a waltz. Amers was very fond of the waltzes of Joseph Gungl – a Hungarian who had been a bandmaster in the Austrian Army and in the mid-nineteenth century was music director to the King of Prussia and later musical chief to the Emperor of Austria – which, indeed, are full of charming melodies and rhythms, among the best known being 'Amorettentanze', and 'Die Hydropaten'. Amers gave selections from the newer musical comedies such as *The Belle of New York* by Kerker and of course Romberg's phenomenally successful *The Desert Song*, as well as snatches from the operettas of Millocker, Léo Fall and Kalman. Gounod, Delibes and the other French ballet and opera composers such as Messager appeared frequently, as did many of those light small pieces, now seldom played, by such composers as Leblon and Chassaigne, and Heuberger's 'Im Chambre Séparée' from his operetta *The Opera Ball*.

In the evening the band doffed its uniform and put on its evening dress to become 'Captain Amers's Famous Orchestra'. Each Friday afternoon it gave a symphony concert; Cyril Smith and Eileen Joyce among others made their first appearance at them. On Saturday and Sunday evenings there was an orchestral concert of a light nature usually with a vocalist or a soloist. Wednesday evening's was a popular concert with 'entertainers'. All the afternoon and evening performances took place in the Winter Gardens of the Devonshire Park.

In November 1923, Amers began a series of annual musical festivals which continued until the start of the Second World War. For these his orchestra was augmented to fifty-five performers. Among notable performers was Sir Edward Elgar, O.M., to conduct his violin concerto. Elgar was not a very satisfactory conductor – though Boult disputes this – and he often seemed unable to indicate to the orchestra all that was in the score. A story is told suggesting that he was himself aware of this shortcoming; turning to a famous 'cellist who was about to play his concerto he said 'I am going to leave this to you. I simply can't make head or tail of it.' Perhaps this is why he dedicated 'Cockaigne' to British orchestral players! Eric Coates, at Eastbourne to conduct his amusing 'The Three Bears', recalled that Elgar wandered into the orchestra as he was about to start and sat behind the drums: 'He was quite oblivious of the fact that his entry into the orchestra had created a minor sensation among the audience and that during the performance he nearly dried me up by tapping his feet and waggling his head from side to side, to such effect that it was only with the greatest difficulty I managed to keep my mind on directing the orchestra through the cross-rhythm of the foxtrot section in my Phantasy.' Elgar admired Coates's music, telling him that he had bought a record of his 'Summer Days' and worn it out.

To Eastbourne, too, came Dame Ethel Smyth, last blooming rose of the suffragette summer, and so did Gustav Holst who presented his Fugal overture and concerto for flute, oboe and strings. Joseph Holbrooke – that most eccentric of composers – performed his piano concerto. The great Suggia gave the Haydn concerto – some of the players present remember that although she played the 'cello like an angel she had a habit of sniffing loudly during her performances. Granville Bantock presented his new work 'The Song of Songs'; there was a new suite by Maurice Besly, a Yorkshireman who had been master of music at Tonbridge School, and director of music at The Queen's College, Oxford where he succeeded Sir Hugh Allen, conductor of the Oxford orchestra – he later abandoned the musical profession for the legal. And a new work by Herbert Howells, 'Jackanape' which does not appear in the catalogue of his works.

Roger Quilter, an old Etonian, belonging to a distinctive school of English composers who had studied composition at Frankfurt-am-Main under Ivan Knorr, gave his incidental music to a children's fairy play *Where the Rainbow Ends* and to *As You Like It*. Perhaps the most popular of all Quilter's orchestral music is 'A Children's Overture' which delicately culls the bouquet of old nursery tunes. Others of the same group of English composers who became favourite resort composers were Norman O'Neill who wrote incidental music to Barrie's *Mary Rose* and other plays, Balfour Gardiner whose 'Shepherd Fennel's Dance' and Comedy overture were popular, and Percy Grainger, an Australian composer who adored English folk song and wrote for small orchestra 'Mock Morris', 'Molly on the Shore', and 'Country Gardens', all still popular. Grainger was so determinedly English that he refused to use common Italian musical terms, describing his 'Mock Morris' as 'a room-music tit-bit dished up' for piano and strings.

John Ireland was a later festival visitor, conducting his symphonic rhapsody 'Mai-Dun', so was the great 'cellist, Pablo Casals, who played the Boccherini concerto. 'Symphonic Studies', based on a Giles Farnaby theme, by A. Brent-Smith had its first performance under the composer at one Festival. Brent-Smith, director of music at Lancing College, had written a Worcester Rhapsody and a Sussex Rhapsody, and at Harrogate in 1921 presented 'Barton Fair'. Frank Bridge, another English composer, also conducted one of his own works.

Another great English evening brought the veteran composer Sir Alexander Mackenzie to direct his cantata 'The Dream of Jubal' with the Festival Choir, made up of the Eastbourne

L

Choral Union and the Eastbourne Choral Society as well as the municipal chorus, and such famous soloists as Carrie Tubb now (1967) ninety-one, Frank Phillips – a bass baritone who attained the height of his fame as an announcer on the B.B.C. in later years – and Arthur Jordan. Phillips with the orchestra and chorus gave a group of Sussex songs with words by Arthur Beckett and music by James R. Dear; Bantock conducted his 'Hebridean' Symphony, and Ralph Vaughan Williams his ballet suite 'Old King Cole'.

The 1926 Festival opened with blazing performances: Beecham was in charge. His programme was typical of his tastes – tastes which remained with him all his life: Mendelssohn's Overture to 'The Fair Melusina', Delius's 'On Hearing the First Cuckoo in Spring', Tchaikovsky's 'Francesca da Rimini', the Symphonie Concertante for violin, viola and orchestra by Mozart and Borodin's Prince Igor Dances. At other concerts new works were played – Holst's 'Beni Mora' Suite, the Elegiac Variations by Thomas Dunhill, dedicated to the memory of Sir Hubert Parry. But light music prevailed – John Ansell's lively suite, 'The Shoe', Cécile Chaminade's *Callirhoe*, and Muriel George and Ernest Butcher singing their old English folk songs and comedy duets, popular with listeners in the early days of the wireless. On Armistice Day, 11 November 1926, Elgar conducted his setting of three poems by Laurence Binyon called 'The Spirit of England', including the famous lines 'To the Fallen' –

> With proud thanksgiving, a mother for her children
> England mourns for her dead across the sea.
> Flesh of her flesh they were, spirit of her spirit
> Fallen in the cause of the free.

As the years went, interest in the Festivals flagged and novelties decreased, though the Sinfonietta by the rising young conductor Eugene Goossens was given, Bantock conducted his

'Hebridean' Symphony, Respighi's Concerto Gregoriano for violin and orchestra was played with Fachiri as soloist. Lord Berners's Fugue in C Minor and Norman Demuth got a showing, as, in 1929, did a young English woman composer, Susan Spain-Dunk, who conducted her symphonic poem 'Stonehenge' and her overture, 'Kentish Downs'. Haydn Wood's Variations on a Once Popular Humorous Song and his May Day Overture, Victor Hely-Hutchinson's Carol Symphony, and three pieces by Edgar L. Bainton were heard. In 1930 the exciting 'Rio Grande' for chorus, orchestra and solo piano by Constant Lambert set to a poem by Sacheverell Sitwell was a considerable success.

One indisputably great non-English composer appeared at the Festival of 1931: Alexander Glazounov. Then over sixty, he had performed often in London. One of the few Russian composers to be dominated by Brahms rather than by his fellow countrymen, he was recognised early. He had no experience of neglect or of poverty, and after the Russian revolution he settled in Paris. His last visit to England was to conduct at this Eastbourne Festival – his Seventh Symphony, the Winter section from his ballet *The Seasons*, his Second Pianoforte Concerto, and his First Concert Waltz. (His daughter Elena was the soloist in the concerto).

Coates, once more in Eastbourne, recalls him 'sprawling over a writing desk in the lounge of the hotel where we were both staying, scribbling on a piece of paper, the while puffing furiously at a huge cigar. His bulky frame obtruded through the framework of the armchair in which he was sitting, which looked as if it might collapse at any moment and as he wrote he grunted and snorted like a grampus. I did not disturb him, lest he might not 'recapture the first wild careless rapture' of the phrase which had just come into his mind. So I remained in my chair by the fireside and watched and listened to the great man

in the first agonies of delivering an embryo masterpiece.'
Coates, who particularly appreciated Glazounov's exquisite
slow movements, reports that the composer told him he wrote
his best slow movements under the influence of English gin.

Amers spread his net widely, drawing to his Festivals Harty
and Sargent, Barbirolli and Albert Coates. He performed
amusing items such as the 'Cadet Rousselle' variations by the
four English composers, Arnold Bax, Frank Bridge, John
Ireland and Eugene Goossens; Armstrong Gibbs's 'Peacock
Pie' suite for strings; and a Chorale Prelude by Richard
Gilbert, a journalist and music critic in Eastbourne. But by
1935 the shadows were drawing in for Amers, literally so, for
early in the year he suffered from a brain tumour though re-
covering sufficiently to go on conducting. His sight, however,
got steadily worse. It was the year also of an exceptional storm
in Eastbourne when it was estimated that 500,000 tons of water
fell on the town and immense damage was done to boating and
to promenade tenting. No one had the heart to tell Amers that
he must retire. At last the contract for the provision of the
municipal band and orchestra which he had held for over fifteen
years was brought to an end, and the Council expressed its
appreciation of his work. He died early in 1936: not a great conductor, but a true musician who had helped his fellows and
brought pleasure to a multitude.

The death of Amers, like that of Alick Maclean, ended an era
in the music of the resort and, strangely enough, like Maclean,
Amers was followed by Kneale Kelley who for some years went
to Scarborough in the summer and returned to Eastbourne in
the winter. Now military bands were engaged separately by the
Corporation, which also directly engaged members of the new
and smaller municipal orchestra. Reduction of these orchestras
was the order of the day. Now was the time for big bands of

quite a different kind – Jack Hylton and his large Paul Whiteman-style dance band performed at the Eastbourne Winter Garden in the summer time. In the winter Kelley introduced his Scarborough trick of feature programmes – 'Big Tunes and Small Tunes', for example, and 'From Revue to Grand Opera'. He gave Sunday tea-time concerts in the Winter Gardens providing what the *Eastbourne Chronicle* called 'a bright programme to enliven those hours which are apt to go stumbling on a Sunday between luncheon and tea, and a growing number of people are finding Sunday tea itself a happier affair when partaken at one of these tea concerts in the company of friends. One price of admission to the concert is *3d.*' Kelley occasionally gave new works at his weekly symphony concert, for example the Symphony in C Minor by a Leeds musician called Harding Churton which apparently had been written eighteen years before. At Christmas 1938 the Municipal Orchestra 'went gay', as the *Eastbourne Gazette* put it, in a topsy-turvy programme opening with jolly overtures and selections and following with 'real surrealist music and a-tonal'. (What could they be?) Kelley as Prospero conducted an invisible band of musicians, told funny stories, read some critical correspondence, and led a B.B.C. audition of musicians who could do gardening, play billiards or anything except create melody.

Next month, January 1939, unpleasant noises were heard not at the Winter Gardens but in the Council Chamber. Alderman Edgar Hill stated: 'With regard to the Winter Garden, if I was running Eastbourne, I would pull the rotten place down and built a really fine place, capable of holding really big conferences, as well as making a country club there to which most people in Eastbourne would belong.' Evidently, there would be little place for music under such a dispensation. Music-hating Councillors were no rare species. Even as early as 1877 the *Musical Times* recorded that Alderman Smith, the ex-Mayor of Southport in Lancashire, had a down on that resort's band at its Winter Gardens. The *Musical Times* said that the conductor, Gwilym Crowe,

> having artistic tendencies and being desirous therefore of choosing, as well as of conducting, the compositions performed, occasionally introduced some of the works of the best masters into the programmes. This unpardonable liberty was duly resented by Alderman Smith at a meeting on the subject, and Mr Crowe was reminded of his real duty as a paid functionary so forcibly that we can scarcely imagine that he will thus sin again, at least in Southport. 'What they wanted him' (Mr Crowe) 'to consider,' said the Alderman with much warmth, 'was the interest of the shareholders a little more, and not think so much of the high class music some people puff him about. For himself he could say that he was never brought up in a music shop, but he knew he could appreciate music and he would be better pleased if there was a little more tune in the noise.'

Still, as late as March 1939, Kelley could introduce Benjamin Britten's 'Soirées Musicales', the brilliantly scored arrangement from Rossini's music, and talk of him as a young composer who 'lives near us on the Sussex Downs. He writes music as easily as most of us sit down and write a letter, and he will be heard of a good deal in the future.' But the *Daily Telegraph* complained that 'an annual festival is not adequate compensation for maimed rites throughout the rest of the year'; it objected to Kelley's hotch-potch programmes of such works – 'containing every imaginable cliché' – as Castelnuovo-Tedesco's Violin Concerto.

The *Daily Telegraph* need not have worried: it was all ending anyhow. Eastbourne was practising blackouts in July and August 1939, and when war broke out it was decided that for the time being there would be no music at the Winter

Garden. Kelley, whose contract remained, was to be allowed meantime to accept outside engagements though he would have to return to fulfil the remainder of his contract when called upon. Next month the following exchanges were reported in the *Eastbourne Gazette*:

Councillor Walton: What is going to happen to the members of our own orchestra? Some of them, eight or ten perhaps, are rate-payers and yet they are not employed. Mr Kelley has his contract and his money.

Councillor Wood: What right have we to be engaging military bands when they should be entertaining the troops? The civilian orchestra should be re-engaged.

Councillor Swann said that the bands would not be available much longer for the reason that they would be employed in entertaining the troops. It was the intention to employ a municipal orchestra of about fifteen members....

According to the report of the Committee, the proposal is that Mr Kneale Kelley should provide an orchestra of fifteen players with his own services as conductor at the cost of £95 a week as compared with last year's cost of £180 a week. The orchestra will also play in the central bandstand.

In this much-diminished form the band began to play again, and continued until the Spring of 1941. That was almost the end of it. One bright spark of hope came when the Hastings municipal orchestra, 'after a winter of impoverishment', amalgamated its resources with those of Eastbourne and for a short time the combined orchestras under the name of the South Coast Philharmonic Orchestra gave a symphony concert each week in each town and a Sunday concert in alternate weeks. 'Lighter musical fare' was to continue to be provided by the smaller bodies functioning in their own towns. This too shortly came to an end and it effectively ended the history of the permanent orchestras of Eastbourne.

Way down the Grand Parade with its tall and dignified hotels, past the new bandstand no longer standing on stilts in the sea, leaving the baths and the Devonshire Park halls inland to the right, past the stubby Wish Tower, the stroller comes to a great Victorian building with its own 'in' and 'out' gates standing a little back from the promenade itself: the Grand Hotel. Like many other hotels of less than half its size and restaurants even smaller, the Grand from Victorian days had a trio (often augmented) to accompany the taking of tea in the afternoon and to play digestive airs after dinner on Sundays. It stands out from the rest only because its music was broadcast every Sunday evening for many years on the wireless. By its choice of old, familiar light music, it became a nostalgic beacon, not least to Englishmen overseas for whom it seemed to enshrine one aspect of the English way of life.

At the Grand Hotel the rich Forsytes might have stayed, assuming of course that there were no suitable private chambers they could hire. It was lush with brocades and heavy with Victorian furniture, great chandeliers, and the hushed voices of attentive servants. There the well-to-do Victorian, Edwardian and Georgian middle classes, usually originating in the industrial Midlands or North, came for their placid holidays surrounded by every kind of what, at any rate at that time, was regarded as comfort. Some of them no doubt visited the Winter Gardens and the Floral Hall to hear the orchestra and no doubt sunned themselves on the terraces before the bandstand. But most preferred their music in the tea-shop style, in the hotel's high room with its galleries, basket chairs and, of course, potted palms.

The names of some early players are still recalled: the leader during the First World War was van Leir; Arthur Beckwith followed him and was in turn followed by a once celebrated violinist, Albert Sandler. Sandler was well regarded as a soloist and as a chamber music player but it was not always easy to get such engagements in the 1920s and Sandler was not averse to Grand Hotel music. Tom Jones, Tom Jenkins, and in the 1950s Leslie Jeffries in turn presided. Each Sunday B.B.C. engineers came down to set up their tackle for the broadcast (which probably pleased listeners more than it did those who had been disturbed from their basket chairs).

The broadcasting ended in the early 1950s; symbolic of the era, a Grand Hotel orchestra continued to broadcast – from the studio with artificial applause. As a combination, the Eastbourne Grand Hotel 'orchestra' was a period piece; it has now disappeared along with the palms, and the basket chairs. Today the Grand Hotel is trying to forget that it ever had either palms or 'orchestra', believing that such memories are likely to send clients elsewhere. Perhaps so. In any case, like many other large hotels round the English coast, the Grand's main function now is to house conferences, and to provide rooms for banquets and dancing on Saturday evenings.

Esplanade Weymouth Dorset.

10. Theme and Variations:
Margate, Folkestone, Buxton

Some sparks of sentiment perished,
Some flashes of genius lost . . .
G. J. Whyte-Melville

To the casual visitor, present-day Margate appears to have no history – nothing but the odour of hot dogs and onions, 1,001 thrills at Dreamland, Bathing Beauty contests, the jukebox clack and thump, the wail of Muzak, and the assurance of the Margate Corporation that hotels marked with a certain cryptic symbol **A** in the official guide have at least 'one toilet for every fifteen guests': all the detritus of ersatz pleasure, all the discomfort of reality.

The present obscures the fact that Margate has a longer history as a resort than most. Visitors flocked here from the late eighteenth century when doctors blessed sea-bathing; its Assembly Rooms (dances eight to midnight) opened in 1769

when George III was an upstanding, happy young monarch; it
had Tivoli Gardens (originally Shady Grove Tea Gardens)
for forty years from 1829, providing public breakfasts, concerts,
musical promenades, comics, and ballads by Miss Jacobs whose
'eyes were black as blots'.

Before 1838, Surtees tells us in *Jorrocks's Jaunts and Jollities*,
gay Londoners of the lower middle class sent their families for
a fortnight at Margate, the bread-winner joining them for the
weekend via the 'husbands' boat' from Tilbury in which *en
voyage* they danced to a band of harp, flute, lute, big horn and
short horn. When they landed, in their dark blue stocking
pantaloons, kerseymere waistcoats, velvet caps with tassels,
what reunions on the jetty while the Town Band played
popular operatic airs! And, observes Lord William Pitt
Lennox in 1857, everyone – gay ladies, antiquated dames in
bathchairs, 'would-be-yachtsmen' in duck trousers, middle-
aged females 'got up in the most juvenile manner with
knowing hats and short petticoats' and cigar-smoking
cavaliers – is delighted with music when they can have it for
nothing.

'Animated' sea-bathing from rooms where pianos played
with 'a rich banjo tune'; streets thronging with goat and
donkey drivers, shoeblacks, saleswomen offering laces, anti-
macassars, crochet work, vendors of Bath buns, pologne-
sausages, brandy balls, imperial pop, periwinkles, roast
potatoes, fishermen crying lobsters, Pegwell Bay prawns and
mackerel 'all alive'! In the Assembly Rooms, Genge, the
sweetest of tenors; metropolitan stars at the Theatre Royal;
elephants, acrobats, female equestrians at the American
Circus; and the largest stuffed pig in the world to be seen at the
Dog and Duck.

And with it all, music, music everywhere. Too much for
some. In 1859 Margate Town Council issued a by-law: 'In case

any street musician shall not depart from the neighbourhood of any dwelling house on being required so to do by the occupier . . . he shall forfeit any sum not exceeding 20*s*' (i.e. £6 today). What made it worse was its inclusion in by-laws relating to 'Street Cleansing and the Removal of Refuse'. The secret – and not so secret – antipathies of local Councillors for music is a continuous theme of our story.

Nevertheless by the 1890s the Borough was proffering concerts in the season by 'The Corporation Band' which was Herr Moritz Würm's 'Red Viennese Band', leader Herr Krammer. Würm, with a Kaiser-style moustache and a manner to match, appeared only after the first item. Usually he played a violin solo during the concert. His band was composed of strings, woodwind, brass and piano and, despite its conductor and leader, was largely composed of English instrumentalists. Its members wore blue uniforms trimmed with red and gold braid, and they played three times a day at the Oval, the Park and the Fort except for Monday and Thursday afternoons when they were free. Their programmes included Strauss waltzes, overtures by Beethoven, Suppé, and Auber, selections from Victor Herbert's musical comedies – and in July 1901 a Galop by Oser called 'Influenza', an intriguing title but scarcely good public relations for Margate.

The Jorrocks's spirit persisted: when the band played dance music, some of the audience so far forgot that the twentieth century was nearly upon them as to leap to their feet and dance around the bandstand. But why not? Dance music (or some of it) is for dancing, and how better to cure the cramp from hard seats than to dance during a concert? There is nowhere in England now where, after enjoying Beethoven or Wagner, one can seize one's partner and whirl round the band (though they still do it in France and Germany).

Würm departed for Folkestone in 1903 and was succeeded

by Karoly Klay and his Blue Hungarian Band.[1] One evening
Klay was given a message that 'Peace is Proclaimed'. At once
he led his Blue Hungarians into a triumphal march (identity
unrevealed). It was the end of the Boer War. A season or two
later came the 'Royal Meister' Orchestra. This marked a
turning point. Its conductor was Edmund Maney, a violinist
in the newly-formed (1904) London Symphony Orchestra,
seceded from the Queen's Hall Orchestra because of Wood's
insistence on 'no deputies at rehearsals'. Two other brothers
Maney were in the orchestra, originally of seventeen players,
all with London experience. Before long, under the guidance
of John E. Saxby, secretary to the 'Fêtes Committee' and later
Entertainments Manager, the 'Royal Meister' became the
Margate Municipal Orchestra, its size increasing to twenty-
five, then thirty-six and in August forty-one. At night ambitious
classical programmes were presented, such members as Alfred
Barker and Aubrey Brain performing concerti.

The Corporation, believing that 'The orchestral and higher
class of music must be considered as one of the necessary
amenities of a health resort', agreed to a $1d$ band rate; so
successful, however, were Maney's concerts that it was never
levied. In 1911 the band for the first time was given an indoor
place in which to play – the Pavilion and Winter Gardens,
built at a cost of £26,000. And now soloists were liberally
engaged – Tettrazini, Melba, Clara Butt, Kreisler, Backhaus.
In 1923, despite a lull during the First World War when a
Private James Edgar formerly of the Scottish Orchestra
conducted local and army musicians, no less than £52,000
from the takings of Margate entertainments had gone to
relieve the rates: an astonishing feat.

After the war, the Municipal Orchestra was reformed under

---

[1] There was also a Herr Delicat who, while conducting, slowly turned from
facing his band to facing his audience. This was in Margate, date unknown.

G. Bainbridge Robinson, the stocky, energetic clarinettist from Bath. Success continued; such enthusiasm was there that some amateurs were allowed to sit – not playing – with the back row of violinists, and a certain young oboist, Terence McDonagh sat next to the celebrated John Field to 'watch the part'.[1] Bainbridge Robinson was a sound musician and a good director, and he engaged such fine musicians as Leonard Hirsch – playing in his vacation from the Manchester Royal College of Music[2] – the timpanist James Bradshaw (later chosen by Beecham for the Royal Philharmonic Orchestra), and the greatest of all timpanists, Gezink. His orchestra varied in number between twenty and thirty-five, being augmented in the evening by Frederick Stock (not the celebrated Chicago conductor) and his octet and Charles Ambler's band, which during the day played elsewhere on the sea-front. Robinson sought to establish a weekly symphony concert, but without much success. It was cheaper to go to London. In those days, the 1920s, Margate to London was 5*s* return and a seat at the Sunday League concert at the Palladium to hear the New Symphony Orchestra under Sir Landon Ronald cost 1*s* 2*d* or 1*s* 6*d*.

Much more successful were Robinson's Musical Festivals, usually held in mid-September at the end of the season, with the Municipal Orchestra augmented to fifty. There were guest conductors, Beecham being advertised twice though never appearing; but Landon Ronald, Cowen and Sargent conducted. Gustav Holst presented his own 'Beni Mora' and 'The Perfect Fool', and Eric Coates, Wilfrid Sanderson and Albert W. Ketelbey directed their works. Suggia gave the Haydn 'Cello

[1] He also won first prize at 'Uncle Mac's' nigger minstrel show on the sands for his performance of 'Yes, we have no bananas'.

[2] Hirsch, now conductor of the New B.B.C. Orchestra, and a Professor at the Royal College in London, was in the Hallé and Leader of the Philharmonia. For a time in the 1930s he led the Buxton Municipal Orchestra.

Concerto, William Primrose the Tchaikovsky Violin Concerto (this was before he specialised in the viola), Isolde Menges the Bruch Concerto; and such now-forgotten instrumentalists as Sheridan Russell ('cello) and Ivan Phillipowsky performed. As late as 1923 the 'full Municipal Orchestra' accompanied the presentation of films – Douglas Fairbanks in *Robin Hood* for example – and also, as part of the Festival linked a ballad concert, a form of entertainment then dying in London. What was a ballad concert programme, now only a memory of the aged, really like? This one at the Winter Gardens, Margate, at 8.15 on Sunday, 16 September 1923, began with the Overture 'Fingal's Cave' then Olive Sturgess (soprano) in John Ireland's 'Spring Sorrow' (words by Rupert Brooke) and W. Merse-Rummel's 'Ecstasy', words by an unknown author –

> Mount, my soul, and sing at the height
> Of thy clear flight in the light and the art,
> Heard or unheard in the light,
> Sing there, sing there.

After 'Le Rouet d'Omphale', Herbert Heyner sang an aria from Federico Ricci's *La Prigiorne di Edimburgo* – composed in 1838 and based on Scott's *Heart of Midlothian* – and Olga Haley the Bohemian Love Song from *Carmen*. Other solo songs were Richard Hayemen's 'At the Well' (words by Tagore), Easthope Martin's 'The Last Fairing' and 'Cargoes' (Masefield), Frank Bridge's 'O, That it Were So' and Kennedy Fraser's 'Eriskay Lullaby'. Mackenzie's orchestral prelude 'Columba' ended the concert. In the other Festival programmes there were few real novelites – apart from Kalinnikov's first Symphony, written nearly forty years before, D'Indy's 'La Forêt Enchantée' or a local item the 'Daphne and Peneus' overture by Dr Haigh, formerly a choirmaster in Ramsgate.

Even this enterprise faded and Robinson departed in 1928 to be followed by Herbert Lodge, a fine bass player with a delight in chamber music. After leaving the Royal Academy, he studied in Berlin, playing at the Kroll Opera House and later served in the Army in Ireland during the Rebellion. He claimed to be the first bass player to broadcast a solo, to feature in a talking picture, and to make a gramophone record. His experience ranged from the Royal Philharmonic Orchestra to a circus. He appeared at London cinemas with an all-saxophone band. Short, dark and dapper, he was well equipped for Margate in the 1930s. He played light classical concerts in the open air at the Oval on Friday mornings but the need for 'novelties' pursued him like the Furies, his orchestra being required to sing, dance and play comedy duets. One novel duet for violin (Mac Saunders) and double bass (William Colborne) was a 'vamp' in the course of which, according to the *Thanet Gazette*, 'much amusement is caused by the reaction of other members of the orchestra who become bored and indulge in games of cards, smoking or reading their newspapers, much to the disgust of the soloists'. Next day the orchestra played the Schumann Piano Concerto and the 'Unfinished' Symphony. Among his players were, still, Leonard Hirsch – who by this time had formed the Hirsch Quartet in Manchester where he played during the winter with the Hallé – and the leading 'cellist Stuart Knussen. At Margate Hirsch led a section of the orchestra called the London Novelty Sextet; and with the orchestra accompanied, on Sunday evenings during a musical programme, comedians such as John Tilly, Gillie Potter and Layton and Johnstone. What contrasts! Friday mornings at the Oval, Hirsch, Wayne and Knussen played Schubert's Trio in B Flat; Friday evenings, 'Have You Ever Been Lonely?' and 'Sittin' in the Dark'.

The war ended all that, but the Municipal Orchestra reformed under Lodge in 1946. It lasted only a season and Lodge departed – without either the usual bang or a noticeable

34. 'A cast-iron erection like a bird cage on stilts': Grand Parade
bandstand, Eastbourne, about 1894

35. The Duke of Devonshire's Eastbourne Orchestra, Pierre Tas
conducting, early 1900s

36. *Male soprano, Venanzio Rauzzini, musical director at Bath from 1781 to 1810. A tablet commemorates him in Bath Abbey where he is buried*

37. *Every evening from 7 to 9.30, 'all the most celebrated and scientific [sic] compositions' at the Montpellier Rotunda, Cheltenham Spa, about 1825*

whimper – to Worthing. Quintets were engaged instead, and during the winter the London Philharmonic gave six concerts, as it still does. These concerts cost £1,000 each; the Arts Council provides £550 and the door takings amount to about £450. Of course, it is much cheaper. The cost of running even a modest Municipal Orchestra for a short summer season would be at least six times that sum. But it is odd that while, in the Sunshine Theatre of Dreamland, Old Tyme Music Hall flourishes, old time Municipal Orchestra is thought impossibly unappealing.

One man – a rather retiring man – put the well-groomed Kentish resort of Folkestone on the musical map. His name was James William Eldridge Newman, and he came to a melancholy, enigmatic end when he was fifty-one. Eldridge Newman spent twelve years in Folkestone, from 1928–40: it was the only period when the town emerged from the ruck of resort orchestras.

Before him, from at least 1868 there had been a Town Band of brass and strings playing on the suavely elegant Leas; the usual foreign performers, the Kossuth Hungarian Band, military bands on the Victorian Pier and the Leas bandstands; and in the early 1920s two 'Amusements Association Bands' under Prickett and Stratford and in the Marine Gardens G. E. Cooper and his orchestra. In 1927, the Leas Cliff Hall, costing £90,000 with its roof at road level and its three storeys perched on the cliff side, was opened by Prince Henry, Duke of Gloucester, who declared it to be 'the most palatial concert hall in England', after which the newly-formed Municipal Orchestra, with the Folkestone Male Voice Choir, performed Gounod's 'Hymn to Apollo' and Elgar's 'Pomp and Circumstance March No. 1'. Organ, celesta, tubular bells and piano were bought and Captain Algernon Holland was appointed Musical Director of the twenty-five-piece orchestra at a salary of £20 a month, to provide sixteen concerts a week throughout the year, each player being paid about £15 a month. The parks superintendent went to Belgium to select suitable palms for the Hall. Two dozen ornamental flower pots – twelve blue, twelve gold – were purchased, and an anvil was lent to the orchestra, presumably to be employed in Wagner's and Tchaikovsky's works. But, though (or perhaps because) a yearly subscription cost only three guineas,[1] the new Hall lost money, takings being £6,000 by January 1927, against an expenditure of £15,000. Also the musicians, especially Captain Holland, were dissatisfied with their pay, in which dissatisfaction they were supported by the Folkestone and District Trades Council. There were some other minor pinpricks. Captain Holland complained that the noise occasioned by the serving of refreshments in the Hall caused annoyance. The chairs were not irreproachable: a Dr Fulton, staying at the Carlton Hotel, complained that his wife's chair collapsed, causing her injury – the Entertainments Committee refused liability but extended their sympathy to Mrs Fulton.

Whether or not all or any of the financial loss could be laid at Captain Holland's door, in May 1928 his place was taken by Eldridge Newman, at a salary of £750 a year, a considerable advance on that of his predecessor. Newman, born at Wood Green in Essex in 1889, had broken off his career as an orchestral violinist in 1915 to join the Inns of Court Regiment and had been commissioned into the Buffs, being demobilised in February 1919. After touring a Beecham operatic production in the provinces, he had obtained the summer post of conductor of the Weymouth Municipal Orchestra in 1925. Under his predecessor, C. Fenn-Leyland, it had been described as 'a full orchestra of first-class London musicians', though it never

---

[1] £1,485 was taken in season tickets, suggesting that there were some 450 subscribers.

seems to have exceeded thirty in number and by 1927 had become little more than an octet. Even so it had some celebrated players, such as Frederick Thurston and Ralph Clarke (clarinettists), William Valentine, the flautist, and Edwin Malkin at the Mustel organ. Newman had introduced a Thursday morning symphony concert with a verbal exposition of the music beforehand and special concerts for schoolchildren – all this up against the rival charms of Don Pedro's Band dressed in cowboy kit. Weymouth may have had good bands in the years when George III's annual visit made Melcombe into Melcombe Regis; otherwise its musical history has been undistinguished.

For Newman, the Leas Cliff Hall – with its reading rooms and subscription room and high windows looking over the Channel – was an opportunity and a challenge. He had twenty to twenty-five players all the year round, money to start a music library (it needed a four-volume catalogue by 1936), and a committee generous in its allowances for outside soloists and keen on music, inspired perhaps by Godfrey's success at Bournemouth. He established Thursday as his symphony concert evening, usually with such soloists as Rubinstein, Kreisler, Moiseiwitsch, Thibaud, Myra Hess, Pierre Fournier or Albert Sammons. Sometimes he allowed audiences in to his Thursday morning rehearsals, or he would play an afternoon concert which contained most of the evening items. The programmes were seldom *outré* but they were given the benefit of careful and loving interpretation. On Friday afternoons in the winter he presented 'Concerts Intimes', largely of chamber music – Mozart, Bach and such fairly uncommon works as a Borodin string quartet. He formed a Municipal Choir of two hundred, gave expository concerts for children on Saturday mornings and of course popular nights, light morning concerts, and tea-time performances while the cups clattered and the audience chatted; even a surprise Vaudeville on Saturday evenings when 'jolly light music' was played.

Newman, slim, pale and restrained in his direction, began to be a name among resort conductors and indeed in wider fields, since the B.B.C. frequently broadcast his concerts and he was invited as a guest conductor to the studios. He was on the select list for the conductorship of the B.B.C. Northern Orchestra in the late 1930s; if he had been appointed he might have still been alive. But, despite some Council criticism, he was content in Folkestone, particularly after he had founded an annual September musical festival beginning in 1930. His orchestra was augmented to sixty and included such players as Alfred Cave, George Stratton, Lawrence Leonard, Douglas Cameron, Léon Goossens, Gilbert Winter, Frederick Riddle and Tina Bonifacio. Wood, Harty, Beecham, Barbirolli came; so did Elgar, Goossens, Coates, Dame Ethel Smyth and Susan Spain-Dunk, who, as in Eastbourne, conducted her 'Kentish Downs' overture and 'The Water Lily Pool'. For the 1936 Festival, Coates composed his 'Saxo-Rhapsody' which was played by Sigurd Rascher – he also performed Lars-Erik Larsson's saxophone concerto – and Newman gave his own 'Dorset Suite' whose final movement, 'The Old Josser's Dance', became very popular.[1] Newman's organ player, Clifton Parker, was a neo-Delian composer whose works, for example his 'Willow Pattern' ballet and his Rumba for piano and orchestra, seldom failed to appear on Folkestone programmes.

But the chill winds, never far away in Folkestone, began to blow into the Leas Cliff Hall, and on to Newman's symphony concerts and 'Concerts Intimes'. The public grew cold and the committee became more stringent in their financial allocations,

---

[1] In 1935, at the Wigmore Hall, there was a recital of Newman's works, including his orchestration of some of Cyril Scott's piano pieces, and his 'Pamela' waltz.

refusing to underwrite any augmentation of the orchestra. In 1939 it was reduced to an octet with Newman as a playing member. In May 1940 he rejoined the Buffs he had left twenty-one years before and as a Second Lieutenant found himself helping to guard Folkestone harbour during the retreat from Dunkirk. A little later, aged fifty-one, he was posted to a secret establishment at another Dunkirk, the one near Faversham in Kent, and was put in charge of its defence.

At this point ugly mystery and swift disaster overtakes the career of this quiet, sensitive musician. It is said by friends – his wife died in 1957 and they had no children – that the establishment he guarded was severely bombed, that he suffered from shock and was sent on sick leave. He returned to duty, disappeared for two days and was found shot – in the back of the head, by whom it was not clear. Another story says that he was in Charing mental hospital for six months, later being transferred to Leeds Castle. Given sick leave, he was taken to Maidstone station to catch a train home to Croydon but was found shot dead in a park nearby. There were rumours of suicide, there were also rumours of shooting by enemy agents. His death certificate shows that he was killed on 15 November 1940, in Vinters Park, at Boxley, just outside Maidstone; that the cause of death was laceration of the brain due to a gunshot wound and that the coroner's verdict was 'Suicide; balance of mind disturbed'. Nevertheless he was given a military funeral and buried at Shorncliffe Military Cemetery at the end of November 1940. He had served just over six months in his second war.

Plenty of musicians, before and since, have taken their own lives, yet there is something unexplained about Newman's death. However it has a certain symbolic finality: never again would there be a Folkestone Municipal Orchestra. What he had created died with him.

Remote, 1,000 feet up, nestling amid the Peaks of Derby-shire, Buxton's warm springs solaced Roman legionaries on leave some 2,000 years ago. Queen Elizabeth's Burghley here drank the waters 'his old crazed body stood in need of', and the well-to-do subjects of King George III brought their over-clareted constitutions for a spring clean by means of a liquid with which many were otherwise little familiar. For them were built the Crescent, the Arcade, the Quadrant and the inevitable Assembly Rooms. What music was then played is lost in the mist and drizzle of the Peak or at any rate unrecorded in the Public Library. We know little more than that Paganini attracted packed audiences in 1833. The Victorians thronged to Buxton not least after the 7th Duke of Devonshire, who as in East-bourne owned most of the land, gave twelve acres in the lower part of the steep town where a pavilion of iron and glass, an opera house – 'the safest and most beautiful theatre in the Kingdom' – and gardens with a bandstand were built.

Into these places swarmed a large 'quality' public of the aristocracy and upper middle classes (whose names were listed each week in the *Buxton Herald*) to see and hear plays and operettas of some sophistication. In 1908, for example, Buxton saw Bernard Shaw's *You Never Can Tell*, Maugham's *Lady Frederick*, and, a few years later, Ibsen's *Doll's House*. Gabriel Fauré's music drama *Pelléas and Mélisande* – with Martin Harvey and Franklin Dyall – was at the Opera House in 1912, so was Wells's *Kipps: the Story of a Simple Soul*, with a curtain-raiser by Mrs Havelock Ellis, 'The Subjection of Kezia'. (What *can* that have been?) Albert Chevalier, Pellissier, Robey, Edward Compton (father of Sir Compton Mackenzie), Bransby Williams, Robert Courtneidge and Hayden Coffin all passed this way; scarcely a celebrity of the Edwardian stage is missing from the Buxton programmes.

Tango teas reached the Opera House in November 1913, and

in the same year 'Kinemacolor: Something New under the Sun' (presumably coloured stills) of the Royal visit to Bombay, yacht racing in the Solent, the Golliwog's motor accident and a tulip study. Naturally there was at hand a fortune-teller, Madame Valentine Evete who, however, preferred to describe herself: 'Scientific character reader, phrenologist and clairvoyant will read the hand. Terms from 1*s*.' At the Old Pump Room, Crescent, Emile Wenzele was available for 'ornamental hair design'; while waiting the ladies could read the *Herald* where there was 'a complete story every week in the season by the best authors; full reports of all musical and theatrical performances, social functions etc.' It was a busy life but only the extreme hedonists forgot what ostensibly they came for – the baths with the natural temperature of 82° F 'fitted with all modern appliances for bathing with either the natural or heated mineral water; also for massage and treatment by vapour'.

Almost everyone listened to, or at any rate heard, music at some time in the day. Apart from such transients as Sverdloff and his Red Viennese, the 'Ellery Band of 48', Blome's Viennese, Stanislaus Würm's White Viennese, J. P. Sousa and his band, and a variety of Army bands, there were at least four orchestras during the season: at the Hydro, at the Empire Hotel, in the Opera House and the Pavilion Orchestra itself. Sometimes they all joined together, as they did at 'a special war matinée' on 26 August 1914, under the baton of Mr W. Iff (before 4 August 1914, referred to as Herr Wilhelm Ifff). The small spa burst with music carried on the rarefied air from open windows and across the fragrant gardens: in the bathing rooms the visitors could accurately say with Shakespeare's Ferdinand 'This music crept by me upon the waters . . . with its sweet air'.

The central musical feature from the 1890s and probably earlier[1] was the Pavilion Orchestra which in one form or

---

[1] That gadabout, Julian Adams, was in Buxton in the 1870s (Chapter 3).

another played throughout the year. During the season of
1898 it had thirty-five players under the Hallé flautist, Edward
de Jong, once a member of Joseph Gungl's band. Some of its
members were great instrumentalists, such as Robert Murchie,
the flautist, and H. Mortimer the clarinettist. A twenty-three
year old violinist, Horace Fellowes, joined them in 1898: once a
programme boy at the Royal Princes Theatre in Glasgow, he
had studied under Hess in Cologne and was to become Leader
of the Scottish Orchestra and of Beecham's opera orchestra as
well as one of the most distinguished chamber music players in
Scotland. Thirty years later Fellowes became conductor of the
Buxton Spa Orchestra. In his autobiography *Music In My
Heart*[1] he tells how in 1898 when he joined de Jong he was
required to play in the military band in the morning; after
one week's tuition he became fourth clarinet.

Concerts continued at full strength during the First World
War, under Sidney Freedman, A.R.A.M., the Hallé violinist,
and there were regular 'classical' concerts with such soloists as
Moiseiwitsch, Daisy Kennedy, the Australian violinist, and
Solomon, aged thirteen (that was 1916). In that year, the worst
of the war, the orchestra was described significantly as 'all-
British'. Cowen and Norman O'Neill came to conduct their
own works. The Belgian, French and Russian National
Anthems, as well as our own, were regularly played. By 1917
Freedman's Orchestra had been whittled down to twenty and
in 1918 Captain William MacBean, 3rd Manchester Regiment,
took over the season orchestra. But only very briefly, for in
May 1919 George Cathie, whom we have already met, became
conductor, with T. H. Morrison – later conductor of the B.B.C.
Northern Orchestra – as his leader. Ketelbey made a début
with a musical joke called 'Mind the Slide', and there were
forgotten pieces by Sistek and Roeckel as well as an overture,

[1] Oliver and Boyd, 1958.

'La Flandre' by Bouillon. Light pieces by Percy Fletcher and Percy Grainger came into the programmes. Complete symphonies, such as Haydn's 'Clock' and Mendelssohn's 'Italian' were played. Cathie allowed audiences into the rehearsals for his symphony concerts – given by an orchestra of fifteen! Léon Goossens was its oboe player for a short time and Frank Gomez its clarinettist. Horace Fellowes was appointed conductor in 1939. As well as weekly symphony concerts, he had 'pop' nights and children's concerts. He often visited schools, showed them his 1741 Cremona violin, and played their requests. Often they asked for Handel's 'Largo' or Boccherini's minuet, but once a small boy asked for 'When Mother taaks in t'washing'. Fellowes was floored; happily his pianist, Fred Dunworth, recognised it as a comic song of the day. Twice a season he gave a Strauss night when, like Willy Boskovsky today, he directed the orchestra with his violin bow, joining in solo as required. Every Thursday the orchestra broadcast and in 1930 held a joint Festival with the B.B.C. Northern Orchestra. One guest was Sir Hamilton Harty who performed his Irish Symphony and wrote on Fellowes's programme 'As classical as Horace and one of the best of Fellowes'. And even in the 1930s, as Fellowes tells us, the patrons of the concerts included the Duke of Devonshire and the First World War commander, Lord Plumer. One night Fellowes's baton slipped from his hand and was returned to him by Plumer who was sitting in the front row – hence the 'rumour' that Fellowes had been presented with a field-marshal's baton.

Fellowes left in 1937 to join the Carl Rosa Opera as deputy conductor to Charles Webber and toured South Africa and Rhodesia, bringing Bulawayo the first live opera in its history. Maurice Miles, mentioned earlier, succeeded him and with the war the orchestra was reduced to minute proportions. It was revived after the war under such directors as Vilem Tausky, later conductor of the B.B.C. Concert Orchestra, and Charles

Haberreiter, who had worked in Vienna with Franz Léhar. Now the orchestra was jack-of-all trades, playing for variety shows, old-time and modern dancing, as well as light concerts including movements from well-known concertos. For the latter the band – three violins, 'cello, bass, clarinet, trumpet, trombone and drums – was augmented by flute, oboe and viola, with parts specially rescored. The musicians were first-class executants and the standard of sight-reading was phenomenal. But, as one of them commented to me, it was an 'eccentric life'.

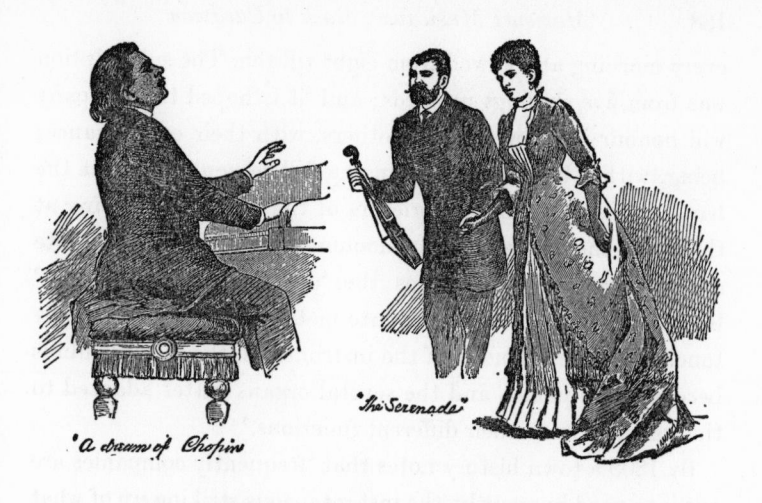

'A dream of Chopin'

'The Serenade'

11. 'Moments Musicaux':
Back to Caedmon

That strain again! it had a dying fall.
Shakespeare, *Twelfth Night*

IN the early days, stray and anonymous groups of musicians strummed and boomed while the water bibbers quaffed their health-giving potations and took their promenades. But what was the music, who the players? At most spas the answer is silence, the records were not kept. Who, after all, wanted to know the names of such vagabonds and the jigs they played? Dr Johnson's attitude to music was common. Some light is, however, let into the dark subject in Cheltenham Spa. As early as the 1780s, soon after George III's visit, the reigning Master of Ceremonies, Simeon Moreau, wrote – doubtless for publicity purposes – 'Tour to Cheltenham' (1783) in which he explains that the Spa Room was open every morning during the season for the water drinkers, for public breakfasts on a Monday from the first week in June, and for balls, from the last Monday in June till the first Monday in September. Music was provided every morning at the well from eight till ten. The subscription was from five shillings upwards; and 'it is hoped the company will honour it, as well as the others, with their countenance; being, with a benefit concert in the full season, and what the band receive from the proprietors of the rooms for playing at the balls, the whole of their emolument . . .'. There is a note added that the music helps the 'operation of the waters' because the 'spirits being put into motion, and most agreeably touched by the harmony of the instruments, the sensible fibres become more pliant, and the several organs better adapted to the free exercise of their different functions.'

By 1803 a town history notes that 'frequently companies are put into good humour by the instantaneous striking up of what is called an organ grinder! Whether he play the tender or the sprightly tune, still is the bosom soothed and delighted. It is pleasing to witness an old, well-known, sun-burnt character, that one recollects to have seen hundreds of miles off, playing the self-same tune.' Organ grinders, hurdy-gurdy players and fiddlers frequently parade the streets of Cheltenham; 'the tamberine is also touched by some female hand, which gives zest to the concert'.

Some thirty years later a band still plays at the Old Well and the Montpellier every morning during the season from eight o'clock till ten. The Montpellier band is claimed as the equal, if not the superior, of any provincial band in the kingdom. Evening musical promenades at the Montpellier Rotunda came in, the band, consisting of fifteen performers, playing from about seven to half-past nine: 'The selection of music embraces all the most celebrated and scientific compositions, as well of ancient as of modern times, appropriately arranged, and which are performed with great taste and ability. These selections are generally programmed before the promenade commences, so that the leader is unable to answer the calls of subscribers for particular pieces so readily in the evening as in the morning performances, when no particular scheme has to be followed, and he is left more at liberty to select, as choice or the wishes of the company appear to dictate.' *Scientific* compositions?

The leader was Mr Murphy, supported by four or five other clarinets; Mr Davies on the flute, André on the serpent, and Klussman principal horn. They were clad in 'Oxford-mixed' trousers, dark blue frock coat, with officer's cap of same colour, trimmed with broad silver band, and white silk tassel, and crimson silk sash. What 'Oxford-mixed' trousers were – unless pepper-and-salt – I cannot discover. When in October the wind and the snow arrived (for it actually did snow yesterday morning, reported the *Looker-On*[1] of 25 October 1834) four players only were retained for the Pump Room.

The Montpellier Band was still playing in 1840, led by Murphy, supported by Cox, Best, Graham and Donegani, clarinets; Davies and Cox, junior, flutes; P. Jarrett, bassoon; Hatton and Cox, junior, trombones; Collins, serpent and opheclide; S. Jarrett, trumpet, and Ryale, horn. With two or three more the band would reach its maximum of seventeen – 'a musical force unequalled by any similarly-constituted orchestra in the kingdom', claimed the *Looker-On*. And what in 1840 did such a band play in May in Cheltenham along the walk so fragrant with the hawthorn and the chestnut bloom, and the bright green hues of the foliage? Here is one evening programme:

March	HOLLONITSCH
Pas Redouble	MEYER
Glee – *The Chough and Crow*	BISHOP
Duetto – *Untenero Core*	DONIZETTI
Overture – *Le Philtre*	AUBER

[1] The Cheltenham *Looker-On* was a weekly for and about visitors to the Spa which ran from 1834 to 1920.

Quadrille — *Eurianthe*	SCHILTZ
Aria in *Masaniello*	AUBER
Fantasia Concertante	BREPSANT
Waltz — *La Plus Belle*	STRAUSS
Finale	DR ALDRITCH

Bishop, Auber, Strauss and Donizetti are well known but who was Hollonitsch, who Brepsant and Schiltz? Other now mysterious composers were Hofer, Starke (who wrote the 'Waterloo Battle Piece, assisted by machinery, etc.'), Burr and Mohr.

Of course, there were other more 'musical' performances such as 'Mr Woodward's Grand Concerts' at the Assembly Rooms and the Montpellier Rotunda with Italian singers such as Madame Grisi, Tamburini, Brizzi — who sang among other things Mrs Maberley's song 'I Wandered by the Brook-side', a first performance loudly applauded by an audience of over four hundred. Liszt came in September 1840, so did Persiani, Rubins and Negri, followed by the Band of the Drury Lane Concerts d'Eté. At the Royal Old Wells the Taylor family played daily with Master Taylor on the harp 'executing many difficult and scientific compositions'. (Again that curious word!)

Apart from really big names such as Liszt, Cheltenham preferred its promenade concerts. Writers waxed romantic over them:

As the shadows of twilight gather round, the Rotunda and promenade room, as well as the grand walk, are brilliantly lighted up, producing a beautiful and dioramalike effect upon the appearance of every surrounding object. So grateful, indeed, is this change of light, that it becomes hard to determine whether the artificial splendour, thus suddenly called into existence, be not more in harmony with the fairy scene than the garish reflections of a western sun. The crowd of fair and sylph-like forms are seen gliding to and fro —

pleasure beaming in every eye, and the bloom of absolute, or the quivering flush of partial and returning health, brighten upon every countenance.

Clearly the Spa's doctors had a hand in this public relations exercise. But so did the head gardener: we read of the lovely flowers 'from Mr Hodge's Imperial Nursery grounds which adorn the parterre, and, in addition to the floral beauties, is an ornamented orchestra,[1] a Chinese pagoda, and an elegant marble fountain, once the possession of Napoleon Buonaparte, which throws up numerous jets of a delicious coolness.' Balloon ascents, fireworks and other amusements were available.

By 1846 there was a full military band of twenty to be heard every morning from May to October, and three evenings in the week at the Musical Promenades, 'which are attended by the *haut ton* of Cheltenham and its Vicinity. Attached is an Archery Ground and Bowling Green, well attended and offering opportunities of healthful exercise and amusement.' Then in 1850 a quadrille band played for dancing during 'the dull and tedious pause which succeeds the performance of a brilliant piece' by the band proper at what were now referred to as the 'Soirées Musicales'.

There were other spas which like Cheltenham flourished mightily but died before the era of big resort orchestras – Tunbridge Wells, for instance, four hundred feet up in Kent, celebrated for its waters and its wantonness in Charles the Second's reign. Its music started in the normal way. In the eighteenth century, the Master of Ceremonies in the Assembly Rooms ruled: 'That a band of music be provided by the Master of Ceremonies qualified to play at the balls, and appointed likewise to play in the orchestra,[1] which band is to be payed in the

[1] That is, the open-air raised dais – an earlier use of the word, more consonant with its Greek origin.

following manner, viz. The Renters of the Public Rooms to pay sixpence out of the money they receive for the admission of every person at the balls, and a general subscription of the company – every gentleman 10s 6d and every lady 5s 0d.'

Writing in 1766 a local journalist, Benge Burr, observes: 'The company usually appear on the Parade between seven and eight o'clock . . . They then return to their lodgings to breakfast, or else assemble together in parties at the tea rooms where it is customary for gentlemen to treat the ladies and their male acquaintances, every one in turn, and frequently to give a public breakfast to the whole company without exception which, in fine weather, is often given under the trees upon the open walk, and attended with music the whole time. After breakfast it is usual to attend morning service in the Chapel. When prayers are ended, the music, which has only ceased during the time of divine service, strikes up afresh . . . until dinner. Dinner finished, the band of music again ascends the orchestra and you once more behold the company returning in crowds to the walks. . . . Twice in the week, that is, on Tuesdays and Fridays, there are public balls in the great assembly rooms.'

But as early as 1860 the glory was departing. Thackeray, writing in the *Roundabout Papers* describes 'Fiddlers, harpers and trumpeters performing in a weak little old balcony' in the Pantiles and laments that the listeners were so few. In 1900 the new bandstand was built on the Pantiles by public subscription – presumably to house the Town Band that flourished at the time of the Tunbridge Wells Charter Celebrations in 1889, and was known in its decline as 'the thirsty eight' for reasons that will not escape those familiar with professional musicians.

The Town Band, composed mainly of wind instruments, in later Victorian times became known as the Ceylon Band. This was because for a brief season it had been engaged for a world

right: 38. 'The last act is always
~~ly~~'. *George Cathie – Blackpool, Bux-
~~Llandudno~~ (right) – with Sir Adrian
~~t~~ and Harold Masters, Manager of
~~Llandudno Pier Company in the~~
~~s~~

~~ve~~: 39. *F. Lionel Johns: 'Idol of
St Anne's'*

~~dle~~ right: 40. *G. Bainbridge Robinson:
conductor at Bath and Margate*

~~om~~ right: 41. *Julius Harrison
high days at Hastings*

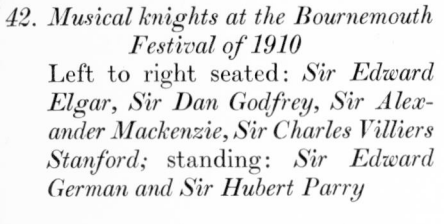

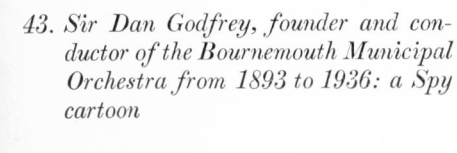

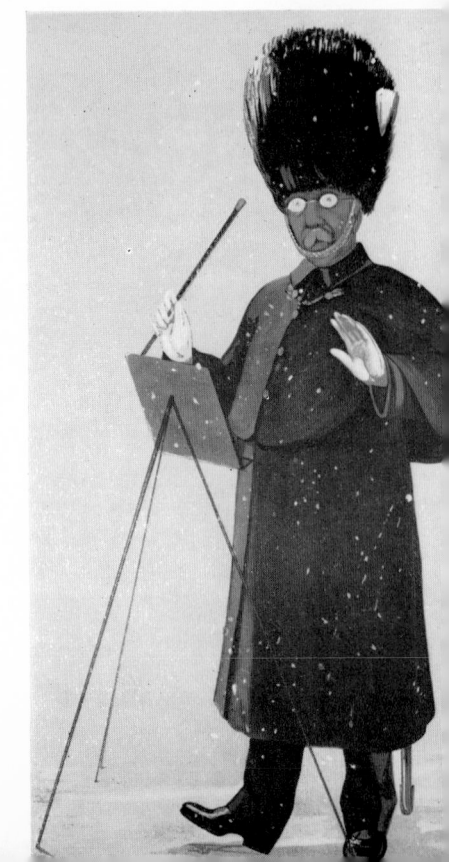

42. *Musical knights at the Bournemouth Festival of 1910*
Left to right seated: *Sir Edward Elgar, Sir Dan Godfrey, Sir Alexander Mackenzie, Sir Charles Villiers Stanford;* standing: *Sir Edward German and Sir Hubert Parry*

43. *Sir Dan Godfrey, founder and conductor of the Bournemouth Municipal Orchestra from 1893 to 1936: a Spy cartoon*

cruise aboard S.S. *Ceylon.* One historian[1] recalls that the band gradually 'diminished in numbers until at last there was left but one – a cornet player – whose somewhat melancholy solos, in weather fair, foul or cold, only ceased when, poor man, he could no longer play. He afterwards used to sit as a model for the students of the Art School.' This solitary survivor, the last rose of a brief summer, passes unnamed into history.

He had, professionally, no heirs; there was to be no resident orchestra in Tunbridge Wells. The fact was that even before the First War the spa became residential and then mainly commuter-land. There were, and are, amateur orchestras and choral societies. The Opera House offered its stage to Paderewski, Pachmann, Hambourg, Melba and Backhaus. The Corporation provided military bands. George Weldon, John Hollingsworth and John Lanchbery have conducted the six annual concerts of the mainly amateur Royal Tunbridge Wells Symphony Orchestra. But the spa opted out of 'resort' music before its hey-day dawned.

There is one place alone in Britain where, musically, time has stood still. Worthing, on the Sussex coast, while still a village gained a reputation as a health resort because of the visit of George III's favourite, but tubercular, daughter Amelia in 1789. Shortly after the pier was built in 1860, nine musicians were engaged to play on it (cost £5 a week for all). The Rhine String Band succeeded them. In 1891 J. Winwood Mansfield and his string band arrived and stayed for eighteen years until 1909. Madame Florence Sidney Jones – presumably one of J. Sidney Jones's daughters – with her twelve-string Ladies Orchestra, and Seebold's 'Chamounix' Orchestra (earlier known as 'The Swiss Band' or 'The Jungfrau Kapelle') also played at

---

[1] Charles Hilbert Strange in *The Jubilee of Tunbridge Wells as an Incorporated Borough* (1939).

Worthing. Seebold built the Dome and became a cinema proprietor; Mansfield, proprietor of a music shop, started children's concerts and organised chamber music.

It was only after the opening in 1926 of the Pier Pavilion at the shore end of the pier that municipal music began, at first under Joseph Shadwick with an octet, then with the same forces directed by Dr John A. Heuvel and, in 1935 – winters only – with Herbert Lodge's twelve players, who spent the summers at Margate. Like his predecessor Lodge was obliged to augment his team with amateurs to play classical concerts on the first and third Thursdays of each month. For these concerts he engaged young soloists, Sir Henry Wood and the inevitable Eric Coates.

Under Lodge the Municipal Orchestra broadcast frequently and gained some renown. It was reformed after the war – which Lodge spent as musical adviser to E.N.S.A. in Southern Command – but it lost money steadily until 1954 when Lodge retired from ill-health and was succeeded by James Kershaw with an octet which remains to this day with the title of Worthing Municipal Orchestra – the only one left. Whether eight players can strictly speaking be called an 'Orchestra' is a question. But Worthing has never had much more and Kershaw (now an all-the-year musical director) continues to augment from the amateur Citizens Orchestra founded by Lodge so that Celebrity Concerts are possible, symphony concerts are given – even in recent years including the second performance in the world of Alan Bush's Piano concerto. As in the past, however, the staple fare is 'Palm Court'. Between the Rhine String Band and the Municipal Orchestra of today time has stood still.

Brighton has always been 'different' – often eccentrically so, as anyone catching his first glimpse of the Prince Regent's

Pavilion realises quite forcibly. With its Regency background it might be thought to have had a strong, continuous musical tradition, but it has not. Its music, like Zimri, has been 'everything by starts and nothing long'. From 1870 it had yearly festivals run by the Czech pianist, Wilhelm Kuhe, who commissioned new works and put Brighton on the musical map – but the festival vanished in 1882, despite the *Musical Times* remonstrance that it had been 'a large-scale event of high importance'. From 1909 it had a Municipal Orchestra under Joseph Sainton which revived the annual festival and even brought the 'Brighton Festival Chorus' to London to sing the Verdi Requiem.

For ten years, from 1914, the Municipal Orchestra was conducted by an extraordinary man, six foot tall and very broad with a mane of white hair, sometimes tinged with primrose, called Henry Lyell-Taylor. Outdoors he wore a fur-trimmed coat with a huge beaver collar. His dress-suit was perfectly cut and his shirt-front was adorned with diamond studs. A violinist from the Midlands, he had been Wood's leader, sometimes conducting the second part of the 'Proms'. He had conducted at Colwyn Bay and Buxton. At Brighton he performed, mainly on the West Pier, a variety of music including symphonies and concerti; he introduced the young Isolde Menges to the public, later accompanying her on her first trip to Berlin. Opinions differ about his musical capabilities. Eric Coates considered him an excellent orchestral trainer. One young conductor-to-be, Guy Warrack, on leave from the Army in 1918, thought him showy and recalled that he contrived completely to distort the rhythm of the Intermezzo from *Cavalleria Rusticana*. That he was 'temperamental' there is no doubt, which is perhaps why the 'ladies' adored him. He was said to bring his sheepdog to his pier concerts where it sang the National Anthem to the orchestra's accompaniment. Lyell-

Taylor was appointed conductor of the Durban Municipal Orchestra in 1924 and remained in South Africa the rest of his long life. With his departure a Municipal Orchestra as such lapsed though there were Pier Orchestras, one conducted for a short time by Julian ('Midge') Clifford, jnr, whom we glimpsed earlier billed at Harrogate as the youngest conductor in the world; another on the Palace Pier was directed by Jimmy Sale from the Palladium.

In 1929 the Corporation decided after all to have a Municipal Orchestra, an all-the-year round one, though bigger in winter (twenty-eight) than in the summer (eighteen). Jan Hurst was appointed director and the concerts were launched with high hopes. Hurst was delighted and quickly became a popular figure, 'a master of elegance' one journalist described him and another wrote of his graceful figure waving his baton from his finger tips 'with flourishes and gambits and various departures from the orthodox orbit of the conductor's wand ... significant waving of both hands from the wrists'. (Musicians agree that his stick technique was first-class.)

All too quickly difficulties began. The Aquarium was neither an entirely suitable concert hall nor were its acoustics tolerable. Beecham, a guest conductor, after congratulating the orchestra on its fine playing, castigated the building, the result being that Hurst was slated by the Entertainments Committee. Another snag was the adverse attitude of the officials. The orchestra was scarcely advertised at all – Sir Henry Wood, another visiting conductor, was angry at the lack of bill posters advertising his appearance. It was the gradual squeezing by officials and the Committee that led to the orchestra's extinction. At the time, 1934, Elgar was visiting to conduct some of his works: on hearing the news, he waxed publicly wrathful against the Council and its Committee. But to no avail. To no avail, either, the cutting remarks of the newspapers. The *Music-Lover*, a popular music journal of the time, wrote: 'Brighton to its ever-lasting shame has been completely devoid of orchestral music' since the orchestra was ended – or rather since the Corporation 'ran away'. The paper added 'We would point out to these ante-diluvian assessors that they are already paying out money for the weeding of their gardens and incredibly as it may seem they presumably have occasion to engage painters and decorators to prop up the Dome. Public gardens do not make profits any more than orchestras' – exactly the argument that had been used in Harrogate.

Two small, snide memories Hurst could not forbear recalling – and who shall blame him? The first was of a long-winded Councillor saying, 'We look in our programmes and we not only have the names of the compositions but we also have got anaesthetical notes'; the other was of a Councillor at a committee meeting asking those present to stand up in silence in memory of the passing of a Royal personage and announcing that the meeting would close with the Rev. —— 'pronouncing Benedictine'.

This is the last time we shall meet Jan Hurst in this book or in life, for he died in 1967, the last of the conductors whose life work was with the resort orchestras. Coming from a family of watch and clockmakers in Lancashire, he had played in his father's amateur orchestra, was taught by Egon Petri, played the organ in a Swedenborgian Church when he was twelve and toured with Adeler and Sutton's pierrots when he was fourteen. Soon he gave up his labours at his father's bench and went to London. He accompanied the famous violinist Szigeti; he worked with Gomez, a Spanish violinist who had been Court violinist to the King of Spain; he toured with Clara Butt – and found it 'a terrible struggle' to make ends meet. After spells at Scarborough and Eastbourne as an orchestral pianist, he joined the Army in the R.A.S.C. Mechanical Transport Section, and was put in charge of entertainments with a fine orchestra of forty, many of them former Queen's Hall musicians. By the time he was demobilised in January 1919 he was a thoroughly competent and experienced musician and was appointed conductor of the Victoria Pier Orchestra, in Blackpool, where he stayed until the 1927 summer season.

In his flat on the front at Weston-super-Mare, with his grand piano, his cabinet of compositions and the signed photographs of Elgar, Beecham and others around him, he pronounced this epitaph on his career: 'In my day, it was a great thing to be a conductor at the seaside. I never bothered to go to London, I was quite content to stay away. I made a living – I didn't make a fortune but I was careful. It was quite a thing to be at the seaside – but now we are living in a new generation.'

It would be ungracious – though it is scarcely within the scope of this book – to omit reference to the one and only cohesive element in orchestral music at Brighton: his name is Herbert Menges. Son of a German musician who started an Academy of Music in Brighton in Edwardian days, and brother of Isolde, he was determined to become a conductor, so his mother Madame Kate Menges, who founded the Brighton Philharmonic Society, assembled a string band mainly from her students and ex-students. It played its first concert under the young Menges in 1925. He is still the Brighton Philharmonic's chief conductor today, presenting half a dozen or more symphony concerts a year. Menges is a fine conductor, well-known outside his native town and particularly valued by leading soloists for his sympathetic accompaniments to concerti. He has the added distinction of being Brighton's only claim to a musical tradition in the town.

At Torquay it is the beginning and the end that are memorable. Basil Cameron, then Hindenburg, became the first conductor of a permanent orchestra in 1912. He had twenty-five players, augmented to seventy for festivals, and members of his Festival Orchestra read like a potted history of English twentieth-century orchestras: violins included Eugene Goossens, conductor-composer; Thomas Peatfield and Charles Woodhouse, both leaders of B.B.C. orchestras; Cedric Sharpe, 'cellist; J. Craen, oboe; Frank Gomez, clarinet; Aubrey Brain, horn. Among the Festival conductors were Mr Thomas Beecham, Percy Pitt, Henry Wood and Cameron himself.

But Cameron was never a good constructor of programmes. The following, played on Thursday, 16 April 1913, at 3 p.m. would be indigestible now and must have been the more so then:

Prelude, Act 1, *Lohengrin*	WAGNER
Symphony in E flat, No. 1	STRAVINSKY
Symphonic Poem, *Don Juan*	R. STRAUSS
Concerto in C Minor for piano	DELIUS
Symphonic Poem, *Tod und Verklärung*	R. STRAUSS

This was advertised as the first performance of the Stravinsky symphony in England and it was conducted by – Beecham.

After the First War the Corporation took full responsibility for the orchestra which was placed under the charge of Ernest W. Goss, F.R.C.O. It went well and occupied a focal position in the town's social life with, from 1930, annual competitive festivals. Reduced during the Second War, it struggled on until 1951 when during the winter an average of thirty-two people attended the concerts.

The following newspaper extract tells the terminal tale:

Silver-haired Mr Ernest W. Goss, Torquay's musical director since the mid-twenties, had his resignation accepted by the town council yesterday. He told members:

'The atmosphere I have been working in for the past six months, the unfair criticism and the underground movement that has been going on against me, has made me feel that I would prefer to crack stones rather than continue.

'Any suggestion that I am a narrow, dry-as-dust musician with a one-track mind is quite untrue. I brought Henry Hall, Billy Cotton, and others to Torquay.' . . . I love a good dance tune as much as anyone.'

But Mr E. Gibbings said the orchestra was playing the wrong tune. 'Mr Goss has got the violins, the drums and the oboes playing together, but he has missed out the one instrument which is very melodious – the till.'

Torquay's orchestra was said to be losing £5,000 a year. Mr Goss's resignation takes effect from next September.

The final obsequies took place on 8 October 1952.

A bright spot musically (in winter only) between the world wars was Hastings, with its twin town of St Leonards, on the east Sussex coast. The towns had the distinction, dating from 1888, of having their own Conservatoire of music, founded by a local organist Dr John Abram, who also organised regular concerts. Even earlier, C. H. R. Marriott conducted a summer orchestra on the Pier while Herr Kluckner and later Herr Würm led German bands on the front. About the turn of the century J. Vince directed the Borough Entertainments Association Band in the Royal Concert Hall, Warrior Square, and in winter William MacBean conducted an orchestra in the Kursaal.

In 1919 a Municipal Orchestra was formed under Julian Clifford, followed on his death by Basil Cameron, who played on the green, onion-domed Pier with some eighteen instrumentalists. Determined despite his small forces to tackle the classical symphonies, he is said to have spent his nights 'soling and heeling the parts' to suit his combination. He was paid £700 for the season in 1923; the same sum was still being paid his successor in 1940 when ordinary players were getting between five guineas and £5 10s and the leader £9 a week. All the same in the 1920s the Corporation was keen on its winter music and in 1937 built the White Rock Pavilion for the orchestra. Though the style was odd – it had red-tiled roofs and a slightly Swiss-chalet appearance, nevertheless it was carefully designed by one of the first musical architects, Hope Bagenal, to secure clarity of definition and to avoid echo. To celebrate the opening – by the Prince of Wales – the orchestra was increased to a permanent strength of thirty-one players.

When Cameron left for America in 1930, Julius Harrison took his place. A Worcestershire man, trained under Bantock at Birmingham, he was forty-five, with experience as an opera conductor with Beecham and the British National Opera Company. In the concert field, he had directed the Scottish Orchestra for three seasons as well as the Handel Society Concerts. He was a meticulous orchestral trainer, a devout admirer and disciple of Sir Hamilton Harty, and anxious to get away from the beaten track in his programmes, whether light or symphonic. Being Musical Director to the Corporation, he could within his budget go his own way. There were twelve concerts a week, two fully symphonic and usually with soloists such as Cyril Smith and Phyllis Sellick, Moura Lympany, Eileen Joyce, Eda Kersey or Jelly d'Aranyi. The Sunday afternoon concert was light classical with a singer who also appeared at the evening popular concert. There were also three morning 'coffee' concerts, usually conducted by one of the violinists or by the deputy conductor, the late George Weldon, afterwards Barbirolli's deputy – but what luxury to have a deputy who was not a playing member of the orchestra! Once a month a 'celebrity' – Kreisler, Paderewski, Rachmaninoff – was engaged to give a recital, or play his own work with the orchestra. For all these riches a season ticket cost two guineas.

The Hastings concerts in the 1930s attained more than local fame; the B.B.C. broadcast them frequently and for three years gave the orchestra place of honour on December 25 after the King's 3 p.m. Christmas speech, then broadcast live and an event no decent Briton could miss, however much plum pudding he had consumed. Harrison himself, though not a great conductor, was held in high regard. He was both musical and literary. Although his finest work – the Mass in C Minor and Major for solo, chorus and orchestra – was written after his retirement from the platform through increasing deafness, his Worcestershire Suite and his Bredon Hill Rhapsody, as well as his songs, had an unmistakable originality. He also wrote a study of Dvorak and of Brahms's four symphonies.

His programmes too, well received as they were in Hastings, even by the 'regulars' who lounged on the sofas provided in the front row, were not run-of-the-mill. Apart from a liberal dose of his own works, such as his Cornish Holiday Sketches, and his Rhapsody for Contralto and Orchestra (and his deputy Weldon's suite, 'Mice'), the classical repertoire was more fully and frequently represented than elsewhere at the resorts, except Bournemouth: Sibelius's Second Symphony, Prokofiev's 'Classical', Schumann's, Mozart's and a select few of Haydn's symphonies were regularly played, as well as Beethoven, Brahms and Tchaikovsky. Concerti by Sibelius, Max Bruch, Saint-Saens (for 'cello), Mozart and Bach, along with some of Handel's Concerti Grossi got frequent performance, often with a member of the orchestra as soloist. Less well-known were Victor Hely-Hutchinson's Serenade for Orchestra conducted by the composer (who also played Beethoven's Fourth Piano Concerto), Lois Henderson's Five Indian Dances from the ballet *Swayamvara*, and Edward MacDowell's Second Piano Concerto in D Minor. Curiously enough the annual musical festival held in February was on the whole no more enterprising

The stress was on conductors, Wood, Beecham, Albert Coates, Leslie Heward and Boult (who gave Bruckner's sixth symphony in 1938, long before his popularity began). That 'contemporary' work, Mossolof's 'Music of Machines', Hindemith's 'News of the Day' overture and Bax's overture 'Rogue's Comedy' were among the few concessions to the new.

Still, each February – a kind of permanent monument to Harrison – a festival is held with a London orchestra and soloists. Otherwise, the White Rock Pavilion and its splendid auditorium has few musical moments.

Many remarkable families of musicians who played with the resort and, of course, other orchestras have been referred to – Dearloves, Nortons, Mortimers and so on. But the most remarkable are the Fawcetts, whose names have appeared in orchestras since the mid-nineteenth century and still appear. They originated in a hand-loom weaving family at Horsforth, Leeds, whence some of them migrated to Eccleshill, Bradford. The family tree (on p. 204) was printed in the *Musical Times* (June 1967).

The tree is not complete, nor does it give much detail of the various members. But Joseph (*b* 1840) was conductor of the Black Dyke Mills band at the height of its success. Mendelssohn in the third generation was for many years deputy conductor of the Spa Orchestra, Scarborough, in which his son Derek also played. In more recent times there is a bass player, Elgar Fawcett, who has a bass playing brother. Most of them have been given composers' names, a habit which seems to have started in the second generation with Handel. Verdi Fawcett (*b* 1869), the violinist, is mentioned by Beecham in *A Mingled Chime* as being his musical factotum – 'as indispensable as ever Figaro was to Almaviva'. Weber Fawcett was for long a Hallé oboist. Fawcetts are scattered through the programmes at

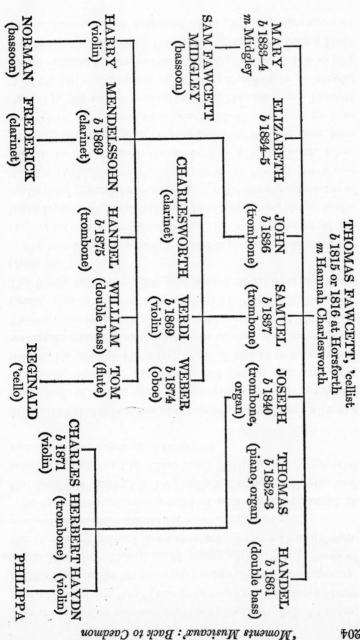

THOMAS FAWCETT, 'cellist
b 1815 or 1816 at Horsforth
m Hannah Charlesworth

MARY
b 1833–4
m Midgley

ELIZABETH
b 1834–5

JOHN
b 1836
(trombone)

SAMUEL
b 1837
(trombone)

JOSEPH
b 1840
(trombone, organ)

THOMAS
b 1852–3
(piano, organ)

HANDEL
b 1861
(double bass)

SAM FAWCETT
MIDGLEY
(bassoon)

HARRY
(violin)

MENDELSSOHN
b 1869
(clarinet)

CHARLESWORTH
(clarinet)

HANDEL
b 1875
(trombone)

VERDI
b 1869
(violin)

WILLIAM
(double bass)

WEBER
b 1874
(oboe)

TOM
(flute)

CHARLES
b 1871
(violin)

HERBERT HAYDN
(trombone)
(violin)

NORMAN
(bassoon)

FREDERICK
(clarinet)

REGINALD
('cello)

PHILIPPA

Whitby, Scarborough, Eastbourne, Bath, Folkestone and many other places. They stand as a clan for all those other dynastic musical families without whose solid technique and steadfast loyalty few of the resort orchestras could have continued as long as they did.

Caedmon who sang his own sacred songs to the harp at St Hilda's monastery in the seventh century can scarcely be claimed as having put Whitby on the musical map, though it is possible that his name will be remembered when some of the town's later musicians are forgotten. From Whitby, where seamen proliferated, Captain Cook set out to discover the Antipodes; from Whitby in the 1920s and 1930s the Municipal Orchestra, during the summer season, frequently broadcast and was heard via the B.B.C.'s Empire service in those same Antipodes and convinced Australians visiting their home land that Whitby was a necessary part of their tour.

Frank Gomez, clarinettist and son of a clarinet player, was conductor from 1923–38. Immediately before him came William Almgill and William T. Ashford, composer of 'Glittering Sunbeams', 'Tears of Anguish' and 'Rippling Waves' whose letter of tender to the Council stated: 'You can have Ladies, Gents or mixed. Terms: 8 Ladies £34, 8 Mixed £40 or 8 Gents £45' – no equal pay nonsense about that. The records do not go back further than 1921, though there had been music for holiday-makers from at least 1890 when Sir George Elliott, Bt., built the West Cliff Saloon. This later became the Spa, though the town was better known for its jet and its fossils, its kippers and its cheesecakes than for its waters. For long there was only an open bandstand; then, when the Council took over, a Floral Pavilion was built round it and later a platform was erected at one end. As at Bridlington, the Floral Pavilion was often an overheated greenhouse, and Sunday afternoon concerts in particular, after the roast beef and Yorkshire pudding, were soporofic, not least for the band.

It was Gomez who put Whitby on the musical map and gained the confidence both of audiences and of his employers. In his first year he had twelve players who, including himself, shared £64 a week – with one benefit concert in lieu of fares. Throughout the period, the conductor had to supply an up-to-date musical library. In 1924 there were to be up to sixteen players in the high season at a cost of £99 a week which rose to £124 next year. By 1931 Gomez was being paid a salary of £15 a week with his seventeen players sharing £118 – with extra fees for broadcasts of 5s for players and 10s for conductor.

Though not a great musician, Gomez had a brisk, efficient way with the lighter classics, even directing with his seventeen players the 'Siegfried Idyll' and sections of Tchaikovsky's symphonies – without a horn player. He had over the years some splendid players in his band – Tom Jenkins, Reginald Stead, Sydney Errington, Maurice Arnold for example – and he possessed a sure judgement in arranging programmes to suit the taste of the predominantly lower middle class, Yorkshire and Scottish audiences of the day. Gomez was a composer of light pieces; especially popular was his pizzicato 'Climbing the Abbey Steps at Whitby', gradually becoming slower and slower as certainly did the pace of those visitors who staggered up from the beach to the ancient, ruined church where once St Hilda was abbess.

Attractive as he was to large audiences, Gomez's contract was allowed to expire in 1938. Some of the reason behind this may be guessed from the speech he made at a presentation to him; the *Whitby Gazette* reported him as saying that 'He had had to put up with a great deal of scandal-mongering and back-biting. Even an artiste was entitled to a private life, but for many years he had not been allowed to have one. He could say that during the sixteen years he had been at Whitby, neither in his private nor his professional life had he ever done anything of which he was ashamed.'

He was succeeded by Michael Collins (at £20 a week) with a band of eighteen. His contract was altered after war broke out to include a clause to the effect that it would lapse entirely if enemy action rendered the Spa Pavilion unsuitable for concerts. In any event, after 1940 there were few visitors and music lapsed. But Whitby had not lost faith in the drawing power of an orchestra and after the war it even increased its size. Under John Black in 1946 and 1947 there were twenty-three players giving regular performances of complete symphonies as well as such novelties as Prokofiev's 'Peter and the Wolf', with Mary O'Farrell as the narrator. Alas for the Council's high hopes! In 1948 a ruthless cut had to be made and Reginald King, a gifted composer of such charming trifles as 'Song of Paradise' and 'June Night on Marlow Reach', who had become a B.B.C. celebrity, brought a salon orchestra of ten with woodwind but neither brass nor timpani. Gradually, after King departed for Bridlington, its size decreased until in 1967 a single performer is left – an organist.

Winter Gardens, Bournemouth.

12. Bournemouth: *Sir Dan Supreme*

O! What a fall was there, my countrymen
Shakespeare, *Julius Caesar*

A ND SO – with a roll on the kettle-drums and a thump or two from the bass – to Bournemouth. From 1893–1954 this Hampshire county borough, which grew from 40,000 to 150,000 population in the period, gloried in a Municipal Orchestra different from all the rest, except in its ultimate disappearance. Different, in the first place, because everyone has heard of it and it is mentioned in all the books about English twentieth-century music. Different, also, in that no obscurity, such as that surrounding the older Eastbourne or Scarborough orchestras, envelops it. All is clear, almost every lift of its conductor's baton being recorded not only in programmes and press cuttings but in such locally-printed works as *Complete List of Works performed at the 910 Symphony and Classical Concerts given at the Winter Gardens, Bournemouth from October 14, 1895 to May 12, 1910, by the Municipal Symphony Orchestra,*[1] and, only four years later, *Twenty-One Years of Municipal Music, 1893–1914.*[2] Nor were lights hidden under bushels, the latter work claiming that 'When the history of the rise and development of Municipal Music in English Provincial centres has been placed on permanent record, Bournemouth will be awarded a premier position.' The orchestra's subsequent history, its 'middle period', is not less well documented, being somewhat naturally the central feature of Sir Dan Godfrey, its founder's, entertaining autobiography, *Memories and Music.*[3] The years after Sir Dan's retirement in 1936 are, however, less amply recorded, mainly because the orchestra went into a gradual decline cloaked at first by wartime exigencies but clear enough in the early years of peace when the players actually went on strike, an event un-paralleled in the history of the resort orchestras.[4] In the years after 1954 it was no longer a municipal enterprise playing regularly in the resort but rather a touring Symphony Orchestra which, despite its musical triumphs, is now (1967), according to *The Times*, 'facing financial disaster'.

In short, the Bournemouth Orchestra's great days lasted little more than half a century, and for most of this time it was under the direction of Sir Dan Godfrey. He made it, his policies gave it fame and though his immediate successor, Richard Austin, was no less competent a musician, the sun was already setting over the musical piers, pavilions, and the Winter Gardens when Godfrey retired in 1935.

Who, then, was Godfrey? How did he put Bournemouth on

[1] Compiled and edited by James Lewis, Bournemouth, 1910.
[2] Compiled and edited by Hadley Watkins, Bournemouth, 1914.
[3] London, 1924.
[4] National Federation of Music Societies, Supplement to Bulletin 4, 1964.

the musical map? And, come to that, why should it have been
in what a Christchurch Cartulary of 1407 called 'la Bourne-
mouthe'? For all this early mention, Bournemouth until quite
late in the nineteenth century was no more than a 'sea-nook'
for invalids, a winter residence for those like Robert Louis
Stevenson with delicate constitutions – for long it had a path
through the pines called 'Invalids' Walk' (it is now called Pine
Walk). By the middle of the nineteenth century a few villas
with ample gardens and shrubberies were built for these well-
to-do invalids who preferred to sniff the pine air in secluded
Bournemouth rather than go to the Mediterranean. It became
a favourite place of retirement for senior officers, admirals and
Indian Army colonels with a sprinkling of baronets and
Honourables. Its connection with the aristocracy and indeed
with Royalty was considerable. The then Prince of Wales – later
Edward VII – the Empress Eugénie, the Duchess of Albany,
Prince Oscar of Sweden, Lord Beaconsfield, Her Imperial
Majesty the Empress Elizabeth of Austria and her daughter
the Archduchess Marie Valeria, Queen Sophia Wilhelmina, wife
of the second King Oscar of Sweden and Norway, all enjoyed its
relaxing air. For all that, *Blackwood's Magazine* in 1881
complained that Bournemouth seemed to take a 'depressing
view of life'. Dances and light concerts were discouraged;
'Dissipation takes the shape of bazaars and social meetings for
charitable objects.'

Blackwood's exaggerated. From 1855 there were concerts in
the Assembly Rooms. An Italian band, migrated from Bath,
played in the town from 1876. Its sixteen performers had all
served in the Italian Army and wore Italian military uniform.
Their only support was by 'public subscription' – i.e. by
passing around the box. A Corporation military band with
twenty-one performers, also mainly Italian, was formed in the
early summer of 1892 under the direction of Signor E. Bertini.

directed their performances twice daily on the Bournemouth
Pier, which had developed from the jetty at which steamers
regularly arrived.

Some eighteen years before, private enterprise had built a
great glass pavilion known as the Winter Gardens at the cost
of £12,000; a skating rink had been opened in its grounds. But
it was not a success, and its shareholders were only too happy
to lease it to the Corporation in 1893, upon which the Corporation decided to engage its own military band of thirty performers. A letter was despatched by the Mayor, Harry Newlyn,
to the most successful military band conductor in the world,
Lieutenant Dan Godfrey, formerly bandmaster of the
Grenadier Guards and the first commissioned bandmaster in
the Army. Lieutenant Dan seldom answered letters. The letter
from the Mayor of Bournemouth was no exception. It lay
unopened on his desk. But he had a son, as musical but more
methodical. This son, Dan Godfrey, Junior, examined his
father's post in January 1893 and came across the letter from
Bournemouth. His father was not interested: do it yourself, he
said. Dan, Junior, did and was accepted. Thus, casually,
almost accidently, the great days began.

Bournemouth was lucky. The young Dan Godfrey, though
only twenty-five, was not only a very competent musician but
a tough, shrewd character. His grandfather and his uncles had
been bandmasters and had played in the Promenade concerts
under M. Jullien, along with such famous musicians as Koenig
– who played the cornet and composed the well-known Post
Horn Galop. His grandfather had been conductor at the Royal
Surrey Zoological Gardens under the patronage of Queen
Victoria in 1846, with a band of fifty performers selected
principally from the Coldstreams and Her Majesty's private
band. Dan Godfrey, Junior, was educated at King's College
School – where his contemporaries included Reginald McKenna,

later Chancellor of the Exchequer, Frederic Harrison, the littérateur and editor, and Walter Layton, later Lord Layton. At the Royal College of Music he studied the violin and the clarinet. Stanford taught him, Caldicott called him a genius and said 'he fairly revels in a score'; another teacher was Sir Frederick Bridge, organist of Westminster Abbey and hence widely known as 'Westminster Bridge'.

He became bandmaster of the Corps of Commissionaires and a little later of the metropolis's first civilian military band, the London Military Band. He conducted at fashionable balls and at Cambridge during May Week of 1889–90, beginning at 9 p.m. and going on until 5 a.m. next morning. During this period, because though tall he was slight, he took lessons in physical culture with Attila who had been the trainer of the famous weight-lifter Eugene Sandow. The training was to stand him in good stead. In 1891 he took a scratch opera company to South Africa, performing such operettas as Audran's *La Cigale* and works by Planquette, Jakobowski, Gounod, Sullivan and Mascagni. Johannesburg, with its gold and diamonds, its very rich men such as Beit, Abe Bailey, Bettelheim and Solly Joel, was learning to enjoy the pleasures money brought, among them opera. But it was a tough and rowdy city with fights, duels and patrons who did not pay. Godfrey himself was obliged to wrestle with a pugilist thug outside the theatre one evening. He says that there was little difference between them in fitness and they struggled until both of them were exhausted, neither gaining the advantage. A strange preparation for the work of musical director at the refined resort of Bournemouth in Hampshire!

He arrived at Bournemouth in 1893. He was to supply a band of twenty-four wind performers to give concerts on the Pier, the twenty-four including enough 'double-handed' players to provide a small string section to play in the Winter Gardens

Pavilion. Godfrey and his military band dressed in discarded dark blue artillery cadet uniforms with gold-laced pillbox hats. Godfrey and his Winter Gardens Orchestra donned a uniform described as 'natty', consisting of a glorified smoking jacket worked with single gold braid and turned at the collar and cuffs with red. Success was immediate. At the first concert at the Winter Gardens on the afternoon of 22 May 1893, 5000 people paid for admission at the turnstiles. The programme included a march, the *Raymond* overture by Thomas, a waltz by Waldteufel, the ballet music from *Rosamunde* by Schubert, a mazurka by Ganne and a selection from *The Gondoliers* by Sullivan. Next summer, 1894, Godfrey became resident musical director – of the first all-the-year round permanent municipal orchestra formed in England – despite the fact that there was a loss of £249 on the first season, the income of the Winter Gardens being £6,227 and the expenditure £6,477. The Corporation, as was the habit of Corporations, promptly cut the band from thirty to eighteen. Still there was a loss. But in the 1896 season a profit of £379 was made, which was odd because the band had been increased to thirty-three performers. Can it have been a result of Godfrey's starting his series of symphony concerts, which was to continue for forty years, every Thursday afternoon?[1] At any rate Bournemouth, and England, began to sit up and take note. Two years later Sir August Manns, celebrated conductor of the Crystal Palace concerts, visiting the resort, was prevailed upon to conduct the Municipal Orchestra, performing Schubert's C Major and Schumann's D Minor Symphonies. Enthusiastically he declaimed the efficiency of the orchestra and suggested the addition of two more instrumentalists; this was agreed by the

[1] The first programme with the orchestra augmented to fifty began with the Festival March from *Tannhäuser* by Wagner, followed by Mendelssohn's 'Hebrides' overture, Spohr's Dramatic Concerto for violin and orchestra, Beethoven's Fifth Symphony, and Luigini's 'Egyptian Ballet' music.

Corporation, and the same year the hundredth symphony concert was notched – and Tchaikovsky's 'Pathetic' was given for the first time in Bournemouth (it had its *première* four years before in St Petersburg).

Important as it was for the valetudinarians of Bournemouth to hear Tchaikovsky's last symphony, yet more important for the future fame of its Municipal Orchestra were two events of 1896–7: one was Godfrey's additional appointment as General Manager which meant that he had complete business control of the Winter Gardens and indeed of all Corporation music. This control Godfrey retained for nearly thirty years; in this he was unique among resort conductors and undoubtedly his shrewd business sense, more than his musicianship, placed the seal of success on Bournemouth municipal music. Sharp, diplomatic and able to talk to councillors in their own language, Godfrey soon held all the cards, financial and musical, and played them to the greater glory of music in the Borough.

The other event of lasting significance was Godfrey's championship of British composers. When he began in the mid-1890s this was a somewhat thankless task, certainly not a policy likely to bring popularity and success to a musical director, particularly in a seaside town. As Godfrey himself wrote, the public had a tendency to bolt when it saw a British name on a programme. It was in December 1897 that the first British composer to direct his own music came to Bournemouth in the person of Edward German (not then regarded purely as a theatre composer: two of his symphonies were performed at Bournemouth as well as his Symphonic Poem 'Hamlet').

Godfrey persisted in his advocacy of British music for the next forty years, the list of first performances he gave would fill a small volume. Perhaps his choice was sometimes indiscriminate – almost anyone could get at least a first performance at Bournemouth – and he realised himself that the majority of his swans were geese. It is easy to enumerate the totally forgotten composers whose works Godfrey played, for example Miriam Arkwright, Percy Bowie, Gerard Cobb, F. E. Gladstone, Harrison Frewin, Cecil Hazlehurst, Algernon Lindo, Ethel Scarborough, Wallace Sutcliffe and Dalhousie Young; and to point out those once known whose works have died from lack of performance in latter days, those Godfrey refers to as 'The Old Guard' – Mackenzie, Parry, Corder and Goring Thomas. More significant, however, are the unknowns Godfrey took up in their early days, often giving them first performances, who made a lasting mark: Bantock, Holbrooke, Harty, Elgar, Delius, Coleridge-Taylor, Vaughan Williams, Ethel Smyth, Arnold Bax, Holst, Ireland, Cyril Scott, Bliss and Goossens. Godfrey introduced to the public the works of Havergal Brian and many others. He was not always happy with new music, believing that some composers were clever for cleverness' sake, that they had no real 'aural' appeal – and in this he was undoubtedly right.

It might be imagined from all this that Bournemouth audiences were exceptional in their love of a continual flow of symphonic and new British music. This was not really so, though undoubtedly the audience's appetite grew by what it fed upon. But Godfrey was far too shrewd a man to provide an unremitting diet of any one kind of music. He was a great believer in mixing the works of the masters with ephemeral, popular music. He was no more above slipping in the latest dance tune alongside a symphony than was Alick Maclean. He even introduced 'stunts' such as a competition for the audience to guess items in a Musical Switch. These, and in the early days, the appearance in a concert of George Robey or Vesta Tilley, reduced the inevitable loss on symphony concerts to a tolerable sum.

The size of the orchestra gradually increased and its military band duties disappeared, a Bournemouth Military Band under Captain W. A. Featherstone being started. By 1935 there were seventy in the orchestra, though most of its daily concerts were given by sections of it. Godfrey became a national figure, being knighted in 1922, and with a regular Thursday afternoon broadcast of its symphony concert Bournemouth became famous throughout the British Isles. Godfrey was a modest, strong man; a firm but just disciplinarian, he was a sound rather than brilliant conductor. Goossens described him as 'jovial'. He certainly mixed well and liked social life, as well as horse-racing, to the pleasures of which he is said to have introduced Elgar. Just as certainly his business guidance (though he ceased to be General Manager in the 1920s) built the Municipal Orchestra into a powerful aid to the town's attractiveness to holiday-makers and potential residents.

Nevertheless what he built has not survived. The Bournemouth Symphony Orchestra of today plays only once a week in the town itself (twice a week in the summer) and is therefore no longer a resident resort orchestra. This is no reflection on its post-war conductors – Rudolf Schwarz, Charles Groves and Constantin Silvestri – who have done much to establish it as a European symphony orchestra of renown. It was the last of the big resort orchestras to vanish; and since it was the stoutest oak in that forest its fall was the sadder. Not surprisingly the thud was scarcely audible.

Acknowledgements

Mrs Lillian Ainsworth; Mrs Sheelah Atkinson; Norman Attwell; H. W. Barchi; William Barrow; Miss D. J. Bartho; *Bath Chronicle*; Leslie C. Beak, Entertainments Manager, Broadstairs; S. Edwin Benn; *Bexhill Observer*; Mrs Grace C. Bingham; R. G. Bird, Borough Librarian, Tunbridge Wells; A. J. Bishop; *Bournemouth Evening Echo*; *Bournemouth Times*; John Bowdler; Bridlington Entertainments and Publicity Department; H. C. Burgess; Ivor E. Burton, Borough Librarian, Buxton; John Burton, Director of Entertainments, Hastings; Francis H. Busby, Town Clerk, Eastbourne; L. J. Burtenshaw; Mrs Maud Carpenter; George E. Clarke, Librarian, Margate; John Coates, Director of Entertainments, Worthing; H. O. Cocker; Arthur W. Cole; R. W. L. Collison; Alfred Corum; Councillor Mrs M. Cottam; J. G. Coxwell; T. F. Cromack; Miss C. Crowther; Colin C. Culross; *Daily Express*; *Daily Telegraph*; Miss Sylvia Darley; Mrs Millicent Day; John L. Dexter; Mrs D. E. Dixon; *Dorset County Journal*; *Eastbourne Gazette*; Mervyn Edwards, M.A., F.L.A., Director, Public Libraries, Scarborough; Sydney Errington; Eric Fenby; Miss Doreen Fennell; S. H. Fewster, Publicity Director, Scarborough; A. L. Flay; H. G. Fletcher, Librarian, Cheltenham; *Folkstone Gazette and Herald*; C. C. Frankland; G. W. Gale; Harry Geary; Colin Gibson; Richard Gilbert; Mrs Rory K. Gillies; Mrs Frank Gomez; Mrs D. A. Good; the *Gramophone*; T. G. S. Green; Stanley A. Griffin; Miss Doris Griffiths, L.R.A.M.; Prof. Patrick Hadley, Mus.D; Miss Alice Hardwick, L.R.A.M.; Dr Clifford Harker; Mrs Julius Harrison; *Harrogate Advertiser*; John Hatton; Gavin Henderson; Leonard Hirsch; Frank Howes, C.B.E., F.R.C.M.; Derek Hudson; the late Jan Hurst; *Isle of Thanet Gazette*; Maurice Johnstone; Miss Marjorie Jones; Reuben D. Jones; Reginald Jordan; James Kershaw, Musical Director, Worthing; Reginald King; J. H. C. Lane; The *Listener*; Light Music: Magazine of the Light Music Society; E. D. Mackerness; Mrs Joan Mayhew; Herbert Menges; Maurice Miles, F.R.A.M.; *Monte Carlo Life*; John Morava; Miss M. F. Morgan; *Music and Musicians*; *Musical Opinion*; *Musical Times*; H. A. Neason, Borough Treasurer, Folkestone; *Newcastle Journal*; Vernon Noble; Editor, *Northern Echo*; J. W. Nunn, Spa Director, Bath; Mrs L. D. O'Nions, Borough Librarian, Hastings; Marshall Palmer; B. John Parsons; John R. Pike, Borough Librarian, Torquay; Richard W. Plummer; H. Porter, Director of Attractions, Blackpool; Mrs Catherine Powell; Sidney W. Price; John Protheroe; H. E. Radford, Borough Librarian, Bournemouth; Hardie Ratcliffe, Musicians' Union; Charles Reid; Miss Lile Retallack; Mrs E. V. Rhodes; Mrs M. E. Rothwell; Royal College of Music Library; G. P. Rye, Borough Librarian, Weston-super-Mare; *Scarborough Evening News*; *Scarborough Mercury*; W. Shuttleworth; J. H. Sinclair; Dr Hector Smith; the *Spectator*; Robert Stead, C.B.E.; Miss Helen Sterne; R. A. Stokes; John Stuffins, Librarian, Harrogate; Miss Gertrude E. Sutcliffe; E. S. Symonds; H. S. Tallamy, M.A., Librarian, Leamington Spa; the late Frank Tapp; Miss Dorothy Taylor; the late Sir Richard R. Terry; Michael G. Thomas; W. W. Thompson; S. M. Thorpe; Ernest Tomlinson; C. H. Trevor; Miss M. Vinall; Guy Warrack; J. A. C. West, Chief Librarian, Weymouth; *Weston Mercury and Somerset Herald*; Charles L. Wilson; Kenneth Wright; William Wright, Whitby U.D.C.; *Yorkshire Evening News*; *Yorkshire Life*; the *Yorkshire Post*.

Bibliography

A. BELT (ed.), *Hastings: A Survey of Times Past and Present*, Hastings, 1937.

JOSEPH BENNETT, *Forty Years of Music, 1865–1905*, London, 1908.

ADAM CARSE, *The Life of Jullien*, Cambridge, 1952.

FREDERICK H. COWEN, *My Art and My Friends*, London 1913.

HERMAN DAREWSKI, *Musical Memories*, London, 1937.

HORACE FELLOWES, *Music in my Heart*, Oliver and Boyd, 1958.

SIR DAN GODFREY, *Memories and Music*, London, 1924.

Grove's Dictionary of Music and Musicians, London, 1954.

SIR COMPTON MACKENZIE, *My Life and Times: Octave II, 1891–1900*, London, 1963.

REGINALD NETTEL, *The Orchestra in England*, London, 1946.

E. D. MACKERNESS, *A Social History of English Music*, London, 1964.

JULES RIVIÈRE, *My Musical Life and Recollections*, London, 1893.

PERCY A. SCHOLES, *The Mirror of Music 1844–1944* (vols. I and II), London, 1947.

CHARLES HILBERT STRANGE, *The Jubilee of Tunbridge Wells*, Tunbridge Wells, 1939.

J. SUTCLIFFE-SMITH, *A Musical Pilgrimage in Yorkshire*, Leeds, 1928.

ALAN S. TAYLOR, *Scarborough Spa: A Brief History* (5th ed.), Bradford n.d.

HENRY J. WOOD, *My Life of Music*, London, 1938.

Index

黎廉圖書社
LIM M. LAI
PRIVATE LIBRARY